YESTERDAY'S BUSES

YESTERDAY'S BUSES

THE FASCINATING QUANTOCK COLLECTION

CLIFF MARSH AND PETER SNOWDEN

PEN & SWORD
TRANSPORT

AN IMPRINT OF PEN & SWORD BOOKS LTD.
YORKSHIRE – PHILADELPHIA

First published in Great Britain in 2020 by
Pen and Sword Transport
An imprint of
Pen & Sword Books Ltd
Yorkshire - Philadelphia

ISBN 978 1 52670 115 2

A CIP catalogue record for this book is available from the British Library.

Typeset in 10/12 Palatino
by Aura Technology and Software Services, India.

Printed and bound in India by Replika Press Pvt. Ltd.

Pen & Sword Books Ltd incorporates the Imprints of Pen & Sword Books Archaeology, Atlas, Aviation, Battleground, Discovery, Family History, History, Maritime, Military, Naval, Politics, Railways, Select, Transport, True Crime, Fiction, Frontline Books, Leo Cooper, Praetorian Press, Seaforth Publishing, Wharncliffe and White Owl.

For a complete list of Pen & Sword titles please contact

PEN & SWORD BOOKS LIMITED
47 Church Street, Barnsley, South Yorkshire, S70 2AS, England
E-mail: enquiries@pen-and-sword.co.uk
Website: www.pen-and-sword.co.uk

or

PEN AND SWORD BOOKS
1950 Lawrence Rd, Havertown, PA 19083, USA
E-mail: Uspen-and-sword@casematepublishers.com
Website: www.penandswordbooks.com

YESTERDAY'S BUSES

CONTENTS

TEXT: PETER SNOWDEN

TEXT: CLIFF MARSH

YESTERDAY'S BUSES

ABOUT THE AUTHORS

Peter Snowden, married with three grown up children, was born in 1952 and a fascination with buses was firmly established from a very early age. The reasons behind this are totally unknown, there were never any family connections with the industry, he never lived next door to an operator's depot or near a manufacturer's premises and had no like-minded friends at school. Over the years, this has developed into a particular interest in the vehicles and operations during the period from the 1930s through to the 1960s. He eventually settled in Somerset, where he spent forty years with the Civil Service working as a cartographer. On getting to know Steve Morris, he became involved with the Quantock Heritage Fleet, including driving duties accompanied by a tolerant wife conducting for him when required!

Cliff Marsh, born in 1940, married with two grown up children, remembers clearly days in the early 1950s when he would watch what seemed to be an endless stream of Manchester Streamliners, Stockport Titans and (then new but far noisier) Stockport utility Guy Arab double-deckers passing his grandparents' house on Workman's Services from an adjacent factory. Grandmother would play an additional role in consolidating the interest - she had realised in that early post war period that companies such as North Western had re-established their express services, and this meant Gran and Grandson could go on the X2 to Nottingham, Grandson sitting on the front nearside seat next to the driver watching him manipulate the controls on an all-Leyland Royal Tiger coach! Early retirement from what became Manchester Metropolitan University has allowed him to pursue his hobby and his involvement with Quantock Heritage.

YESTERDAY'S BUSES

ACKNOWLEDGEMENTS

The production of this book has proved to be an absorbing task, and involved exploring many different avenues, to unearth all sorts of facts and background for the life and times of the buses involved.

This has been made much easier and enjoyable by the willing help and kindness of the wide range of individuals and enthusiast groups we approached for information, who freely gave of their time and knowledge.

Many of the pictures included are by the authors and Steve Morris, or from their collections. Where this is not the case an appropriate credit has been included with the caption. We apologise for any missing or incorrect credits and would be pleased to receive an appropriate amendment.

We are particularly indebted to the Omnibus Society and Mike Eyre for work in providing copies of pictures from their extensive archives.

We would also like to express our thanks to Keith Langston for initiating and guiding us through production of the work, and Jim Yates for helping translate our initial design concepts into computer reality.

Any incorrect statements or details are entirely the error of the authors and again updates and corrections will be gratefully received.

And, finally, to Steve Morris, for what he has managed to achieve.

(Photos Bob Brimley)

YESTERDAY'S BUSES
Steve Morris and the Quantock Heritage Collection

INTRODUCTION

'Yesterday's Buses' can mean different things to different people but in this book we are looking into the history and background of some of the vehicles from the 1930s through to the 1960s, often considered to be the golden period when buses and coaches were the main form of transport for most people and had developed into rugged vehicles which gave many years of reliable service. Whilst beauty is in the eyes of the beholder, many would consider the products of this era to be well proportioned and even stylish, enhanced by their varied colour schemes, lettering and appropriate use of advertising space.

The buses and coaches chosen come from some of the many vehicles belonging to, or which have passed through the hands of Steve Morris and his Quantock Heritage fleet based in Somerset. Steve, born in 1945, has been a lifelong bus and coach enthusiast. Early memories include being confined to bed with whooping cough, watching and listening to the buses coming past the house. The sounds of Leyland Tiger PS1s and AEC Regals with 7.7 litre engines remain particularly evocative to him. Steve's early years were in Stoke on Trent and during the late 1940s and into the 1950s there was certainly plenty of variety to capture the imagination. Local company operator Potteries Motor Traction (PMT) was taking over the operations and vehicles of numerous independent firms. Coupled with this, PMT were also buying-in large numbers of second-hand double-deckers from across the country to replace single-deckers and solve a severe vehicle

shortage. As a student, Steve spent some time working in the offices of PMT but decided to go into engineering, specialising in hydraulics. His interest in buses remained and away from work, his first bus was purchased in 1977; a Leyland Tiger PS1, of course, LFM 302 new to Crosville. Like many preservationists find, removal of panels revealed that a lot of work and money was going to be needed. Also around this time, many of the municipal fleets were selling off their final half-cab double-deckers; purchases were made, rallied for a season or two and then sold on.

Back at work, redundancy loomed – twice – and as a result in 1989 Steve set up his own business, Rexquote, designing and adapting excavators for specialist applications. With the success of this venture, money was available for the purchase of more buses and coaches and the realisation of an ambition to not only own some 'classic' vehicles but to operate them on heritage services or hire them out. With the sale of the Rexquote business, this was to further develop into running more modern vehicles on private hire, commercial, council contract and school services. This has now scaled back to the true love of providing 'Yesterday's Buses' on hire for such things as weddings, parties, school proms and even funerals.

Of course, behind the scenes there has been an on-going, very extensive and costly restoration programme. Over the years, some long-lost vehicles have been returned not only for the public to view but to sample rides at events across the country. So now read the stories behind a selection of them.

The Chester-based Crosville Motor Services had built an operating territory up to the commencement of the Second World War which was as wide and varied as the fleet itself. The early post-war period saw demands on the Company for the re-establishment of services which had been curtailed or limited because of wartime restrictions. Following the reorganisation of bus companies in 1942, Crosville had become part of the Tilling group, which in turn would become part of the nationalised British Transport Commission (BTC). This meant that all vehicle purchases after that time by BTC companies would have to be from the Bristol/Eastern CoachWorks stable, themselves part of the BTC organisation. However, in their wisdom, BTC realised some companies were very short of vehicles while others had comparatively modern fleets. Midland General, the East Midlands based operator, fell into this latter category, and so 35 vehicles ordered by them were diverted by BTC to Crosville in 1949/50. The chassis were Weymann bodied Leyland Tiger PS1/1s, as opposed to just PS1. This meant that they had a dropped rear frame extension behind the rear axle, enabling them to be fitted with a rear boot. In addition, the Midland General order specified they should have luggage racks, thus making them suitable as dual-purpose vehicles. The raised floor section to the rear of the saloon area meant that all seats could face forward, without the need for longitudinal seats over the

rear wheel arches. How near they came to be being delivered to Midland General is indicated by the fact that, on one of the three which eventually went for preservation, under the green paint on the seat frames Midland General blue paint could be found. Their suitability for express work, particularly conveying holiday makers along the North Wales coast, saw them

Above
Front interior bulkhead of restored PS1/1 LFM 320. Top right is a thermostat controlling the circular Clayton-Dewandre heater. Below the thermostat is a circular wooden hinged flap which would enable the conductor to talk to the driver. Three notices indicate seating capacity, 'REFRAIN FROM SPITTING,' and smoking only on rear seats. T-shaped metal frame (nearside bulkhead window) would carry a 'Widd' destination board. Ribbons indicate decorations for a wedding.

repainted in 1952 into the Crosville coach livery. With the advent of newer vehicles, they were repainted in 1958 in express livery, and finally demoted to stage carriage work and painted in bus livery in 1962.

TONY KERSHAW'S CONTRIBUTION

Following withdrawal by Crosville, many would see further service with other operators, particularly for contract work. Seven joined the Horseshoe Coaches contract fleet, based in Kempston, Bedfordshire. It is likely that some of their duties were concerned with transporting Marston Valley Brick Company workers. Judging by the amount of sand which continued to vibrate out of one of the batch when it was purchased for preservation, it probably spent time working off-road on a brickworks site. This particular vehicle (LFM 320) was one of three purchased for preservation from Horseshoe (the other two being LFM 302 and 329) by a long-standing enthusiast and preservationist, Tony Kershaw of Northwich, Cheshire. Over the years, Tony had purchased other vehicles which would eventually join the

Quantock Heritage fleet. Tony's contribution to bus preservation in the movement's early days was considerable. An account in a Historic Commercial Vehicle Club Magazine for 1975 describes him towing an Austin K8 coach bought for preservation by an enthusiast. The vehicle he used was his ex-Crosville Bristol L5G tow bus, KFM 893, which would eventually become part of the Quantock Heritage fleet, along with other Crosville L5G's and a Dennis Lancet coach he owned.

Top right
Having left Tony Kershaw, the history of LFM 329 is somewhat chequered. For a while during 1991, it was parked at Crewe Heritage Centre where deterioration on the bodywork, not evident on the photo. was apparent. It later reappeared in a barn in Scotland.

Right
It was then located in the South of France, being used by a fruit picker as living accommodation throughout the summer months during the 1990s. Having got caught in a flood, the vehicle became immobile until bought and 'repatriated' for the Quantock Heritage collection.

Left
Found in a Crosville Depot skip, a 'Widd' board (unrestored!). Placed in the saloon between the T-shaped metal bracket and the front nearside bulkhead window, the board consisted of destinations sandwiched in what appears to be celluloid in a metal frame. It is believed their use was discontinued after one placed in a box under the nearside bulkhead window in a pre-war bus caught fire, possibly caused by a cigarette end.

KAs, ETEs, STEs AND LIVERIES

The fleet numbers carried by the PS1/1s related to their type and use. During their first (bus) then (coach) liveries they were classed as KAs. When they became dual purpose vehicles, they were reclassified as ETEs, standing for Express Tiger E181, (the type of engine fitted). When finally demoted to stage carriage work, they became STEs, the S standing for single-deck. Initially in green (bus) then overall cream with green wings (coach) livery, on becoming ETEs they were cream down to waist line then green below, reverting to all over green on becoming STEs. Of the three PS1/1s bought by Tony Kershaw from Horseshoe, in 1974 LFM 320 was sold by him to two preservationists and fully restored by them. Apart from major restoration to the body, detailed but nevertheless important to restore the vehicle to its original condition was the return of the front indicator box to its initial specification. This included the fitting of a 'facsimile' green hinged flap which could be positioned up or down to indicate the return destination. The spring-loaded flap was the idea of David Deacon, for some while in the 1950s the Divisional Manager for Rhyl and Llandudno. It relieved the driver or conductor from having to wind through a long destination blind.

Right
LFM 320 is seen alongside LFM 302, on a low-loader ready to move south for completion of restoration by Quantock Heritage. LFM 320 itself joined the Quantock fleet in 2014.

Right
Further work on LFM 320 on joining the Heritage fleet included repainting into Crosville coach livery, re-upholstering and rebuilding the engine.

UPGRADED

Particularly among larger operators, it had been common policy once a coach was a few years old and newer vehicles were joining the fleet, to downgrade coaches to ordinary stage carriage work. However, upgrading was possible on the PS1/1s because Midland General had specified the fitting of boots, luggage racks, and with all saloon seats facing forward. The decision therefore was taken in 1952 to upgrade the batch to coaches by repainting them in Crosville coach livery and fitting the seat backs with extensions to form headrests. Their demotion in 1958 to dual-purpose (express) livery saw the original destination boxes which were vulnerable to water damage being partially replaced, including the removal of the hinged green flap. It is also believed drivers complained about drafts in the cab caused by the poor fitting of the front of the original box. During this time the headrests were removed. All the batch were withdrawn during 1964, some of them having been laid up at Rhyl to meet demands for seasonal holiday camp traffic. A small number were known to have been given low ratio back axles to cope with the Liverpool-Pwllheli routes, although the three of the batch remaining in preservation were not so fitted.

Left
While with Crosville and laid over possibly for a 'comfort break' somewhere on the North Wales route, LFM 320 (KA 244) carries coach livery and head rest seat extensions. No destination box blind is fitted, but the grey strip across the centre shows the hinged flap in place. The number blind is typically set to 'XX.'

Left
At the time when Weymann were bodying the PS1/1s, it appeared they regularly commissioned photographer Charles K. Bowers to record their finished products, including interior and exterior shots of one of the PS1/1s. This interior shot taken when new clearly shows moquette fitted to the backs of the seats. What is not clear is when the moquette was replaced with dark green vinyl as seen in the photograph of the preserved LFM320. Most likely, it would have been when the seat extension head rests were removed possibly at a Certificate of Fitness Inspection.

THE BRISTOL Ls

Above
Two more of Tony Kershaw's Bristols before they became part of the Quantock fleet. LFM 734 prior to ownership by Tony Kershaw had been used by Hawker Siddeley Aviation at Hawarden for staff transport.

Left
Fully restored in traditional Crosville bus livery, KFM 767, one of the Bristol L5Gs previously owned by Tony Kershaw but now in the Quantock Heritage fleet, working in conjunction with the West Somerset Railway at the terminus at Bishops Lydeard.

Between 1946 and 1951, Crosville built up a fleet of single-deckers based on the Bristol L chassis and all fitted with ECW bodies. The chassis designation varied depending on the engine fitted and the length and width of the vehicle. Early deliveries were all L6As., the 'A' standing for the AEC 6 cylinder engines fitted. Later, a mixture of Bristol and Gardner engines were fitted, with designations 'L6B' and 'L5G'

respectively. In 1950, the first 'LL' chassis were received, indicating they were to be the newly permitted 30ft (as opposed to 27ft 6in) length. Eventually, seven Bristol single deckers would be part of the Quantock Heritage fleet. Two would be ex-North Western, and four ex-Crosville from the Tony Kershaw collection. Six would have the rugged Gardner 5LW engine, mentioned elsewhere in the text. The seventh Bristol, Thames

Valley GFM 882, which started life with Crosville, featured on the cover, would be an L6A, fitted with the AEC 6 cylinder engine.

The original Quantock Heritage premises were alongside the West Somerset Railway at Bishops Lydeard Station. One of the stops en route to Minehead is Dunster and Quantock frequently ran bus services to Dunster Village and the Castle.

Above
Fully restored, with additional side mouldings, and finished In Crosville dual-purpose livery.

Above right
KFM 893 while with Tony Kershaw, unrestored, and showing its towing usage.

Alongside the Leyland PS1/1s, Crosville took delivery in 1950 of eleven Bristol Ls fitted with ECW express body work. Essentially the basic ECW bus body, they had more luxurious seating (for thirty-one passengers), and a distinctive livery. As with the PS1/1s, they were suitable for express and private hire work. When the decision to restore Tony Kershaw's ex-Crosville tow bus, KFM 893, was made it was decided to replicate the express style of bodywork. In particular, this necessitated the fitting of aluminium mouldings to the sides and painting it in the Crosville express (green and cream) livery.

It was obvious that the days of the half-cab front-engine single-decker in both bus and coach form in the fleet were numbered when the first of the under floor-engined Bristol LS coaches were delivered to Crosville. They had greater seating capacity and, with their full-fronted bodies, had a much more modern appearance than their half-cab predecessors. However, one more batch of what essentially were half-cab coaches but fitted with full-fronted bodies arrived prior to them. These were Bristol LL and LWL6Bs which became known as 'Queen Marys' Still a front vertical-engined chassis but fitted with luxurious ECW coach bodies, they were used initially on London services. Unfortunately none were to survive into preservation.

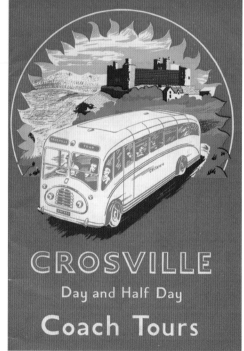

Above
The Crosville publicity department took advantage of the new 'Queen Marys' to feature an artist's impression drawing of one of them on a Coach Tours leaflet.

CONTINUING A LONG TRADITION

Bus operators in coastal resorts around the country have a long-established tradition of providing special services, usually confined to the summer months and aimed particularly at holiday makers. Many such services have been and continue to be operated by traditional double-deckers converted to open-top configuration. For example, Crosville had established the usefulness of both single and double-deck open-toppers in the years preceding the Second World War, using for example Leyland vehicles suitably converted. These vehicles continued well into the post-war period, operating in North Wales holiday resorts such as Rhyl, which enjoyed a seasonal increase in population as a result of holiday camp trade. But, following some similar acquired vehicles, perhaps the most unusual vehicles to be purchased new in 1938 were three Shelvoke and Drewry low freight chassis. These were fitted with ECW thirty-two seat 'toastrack' bodies specifically for use on Rhyl sea front services. Shelvoke and Drewry produced low height small wheeled chassis primarily for use as refuse collection vehicles, but a number of operators had utilised them for sea front services. Unfortunately none were to survive into preservation.

LODEKKAS

The success of open-top services on the North Wales coast resulted in Crosville building up

Above
838 AFM had been painted in North Western livery and used on tours of Northwich a town whose services had previously been operated by North Western. It is seen here being inspected by Quantock Heritage shortly after purchase.

a fleet in subsequent years of some twenty-three open-top Bristol/ECW bodied Lodekkas. Fourteen of these were supplied new from ECW with convertible open-tops, thus allowing their continued use in off-season periods. The remaining Lodekkas were converted to open-top by Crosville themselves and two of these were to join the Quantock Heritage fleet. First there was fleet number DLG 876(833 AFM) and second DFG 81(891 VFM), the latter being one of the last Lodekkas to be operated

Above
838 AFM restored to full Crosville cream and black livery with Rexquote Heritage fleet names. Two open-topped examples, 833 AFM and 891 VFM, also eventually joined the Quantock Heritage Fleet.

by Crosville. Also joining the Heritage fleet was DLG 881(838 AFM). This had retained its closed top but was initially operated in the black and cream open top livery, although later painted green and cream.

Above
Lodekka 833 AFM wandering down the country lanes of Somerset on WSR service.

Right
Lodekka 891 VFM at the Bishops Lydeard station on the WSR, with a second heritage vehicle ex-North Western Leyland Tiger Cub LDB 796 waiting behind.

Crosville's operation of its Bristol open-top Lodekkas was confined to coastal services. The two which eventually joined the Heritage Fleet would see that role continue, but also extended for other usage. That would include providing Free Bus Services at rallies and events not only on the coast but inland, in particular over a long number of years working alongside the West Somerset Railway (WSR).

In the seaside resorts, particularly along the south coast, both municipal and company operators ran seasonal services primarily using open-top vehicles. As with Crosville, both

Western National and Southern Vectis operated open-top Bristol Lodekkas with ECW bodies. The actual Bristol/ECW Lodekka design had been introduced in 1949 as a way of retaining the traditional upper saloon seating layout of a highbridge vehicle (a central gangway with rows of two seats either side) but with an overall height comparable to that of a lowbridge vehicle. The lowbridge body had a sunken gangway on the offside upper deck. Rows of long seats, each seating four people, would be between the gangway and the nearside. The sunken gangway would protrude into the offside of the lower saloon, thus necessitating 'please mind your head when leaving your seat' notices on the backs of the lower deck seats nearest the offside.

From the south and west of England, open-top Lodekkas from Southern Vectis and Western National have featured in the Heritage fleet. Though the Isle of Wight had always been a major holiday destination it was not until 1957 that the first open-top service was introduced by Southern Vectis. Proving popular, during the 1960s, the open-top service was expanded with second-hand vehicles, mostly replaced in the early 1970s by converting five of their own Lodekkas. On withdrawal in 2002, three of them (BAS 562/3/4) were purchased by Quantock Heritage. Their valuable original registration numbers (MDL 953/2/5) had been retained. Covering a large area including holiday resorts in Devon and Cornwall, Western/Southern National's use of open-toppers was originally thwarted by union opposition. In the early 1970s, two Lodekkas were converted to open-top and named *Admiral Boscawen* and *Sir Humphry Davy*. These were experimental models, constructed in 1957 to the then newly authorised 30ft length for two axle double deckers, eventually joining Heritage in 1999, after a spell of service in East Anglia.

Above
Ex-Western National open top LDL6Gs Admiral Boscawen *and* Sir Humphry Davy *flank ex-Crosville 838 AFM, not converted to open top but repainted in Crosville's cream and black coach livery.*

Right
Two of the three former Southern Vectis Bristol Lodekkas which joined the Quantock fleet. They were used particularly on the Exmoor Explorer 400 Service, which included the 1 in 4 gradient on the notorious Porlock Hill.

REGALS, RELIANCES AND REGENTS

Open top single-deckers are much fewer in number than their double-deck counterparts, but two former Maidstone and District open-top single-deckers became part of the Quantock fleet. The oldest, HKL 819, a Beadle bodied AEC Regal 1 dating from 1946, served as a normal single decker for eleven years before open top conversion. It was one of three similar vehicles used originally on Hastings Round The Town Tours HKL 836 being featured on one of the town's postcards. In the 1950s and 60s, Maidstone and District had built up a large fleet of AEC Reliances. Harrington was the body builder for those supplied as coaches, while other Reliances for bus work included bodywork by Park Royal, Willowbrook, Weymann, Marshall, and Beadle as well as Harrington. The thirty-one Reliances delivered in 1961 were fitted with Weymann dual-purpose bodywork, and in due course 325 NKT (325 in the M&D fleet) was converted to open top. Open top double-deckers were operated in the Lancashire seaside towns of Blackpool, Southport, and Morecambe. Blackpool's Leyland Titan double-deckers, with their distinctive full fronts and centre entrance doors, bore more than a passing resemblance to the town's equally distinctive tram fleet. Southport, apart from operating ex-army Bedford QL lorries and Leyland double-deckers convertible to open-top, also operated for a while three ex-Ribble Leyland PS2s converted to open top. Further up the Lancashire coast, Morecambe and Heysham had built up a fleet primarily of AEC Regent double-deckers, and seven of these were converted to open top for sea front services, one of which eventually joined the Heritage fleet.

Left
Maidstone and District 325 NKT (re-registered AFE 719A) an AEC Reliance was converted in 1971 for an additional service in Hastings which was unsuccessful. Withdrawn in 1977, it was with various owners before joining Heritage in 2000.

Above left
Maidstone and District converted both AEC Regal and Reliance single-deckers to open-top. Seen with the Heritage fleet is HKL 819, a Regal 1 with Beadle bodywork dating from 1946, in Bournemouth colours.

Above right
Morecambe and Heysham converted a 1949 AEC Regent 111 KTF 594 with Park Royal body to open top. Following disposal by Morecambe, it spent some time with Southend Corporation prior to purchase by Quantock Heritage and given a red and white livery.

YELLOW BUSES AND QUANTOCK

For many years, the Bournemouth municipal fleet was painted in an unusual yellow livery, becoming known by the public as the 'Yellow Buses,' which was finally adopted as the official fleet name. Equally distinctive has been the range of vehicles operated to meet the needs of this popular holiday destination, and five former Yellow Buses have found their way into the Quantock Heritage fleet. Three Leyland Tiger PS2/3 single deckers were purchased in 1949. Full fronted but retaining the exposed Leyland radiator, they had Burlingham bodies, were fitted with coach seats, and used for private hire, town tours, and sea front services. Later demoted to bus work, they were converted to one man operation, and fitted with bus seats believed to have come from withdrawn trolleybuses. Ending their working days in Bournemouth as offices at Hurn Airport, JLJ 402 joined the Heritage fleet in 2001, with JLJ 401 following somewhat later.

Above
Prior to joining the Quantock fleet, JLJ 401 had been refitted with luxurious newly upholstered coach seats, the high standard of finish of the interior making it very suitable for private hire work.

Right and far right
NLJ 271 was one of six Leyland Royal Tiger single-deckers with Burlingham bodies. Unusually for underfloor engined chassis, but more typically for Bournemouth, they had open rear platforms as well as the usual front door alongside the driver. The rear platforms were removed in 1960 to make them suitable for one man operation and additional seating added. The bodies were also fitted with glazing in the cove panels making them suitable for sightseeing duties in the summer months and this was enhanced by installing public address systems in 1964. NLJ 271, along with another from the batch, was sold in 1971 to Burton upon Trent Corporation for further use, passing through various owners before joining Quantock in 1999. Photos show the bus being restored by Quantock and repainted in Bournemouth livery.

A rather newer bus than others covered in this book, NFX 134P is a 1976 Daimler Fleetline with Alexander bodywork. Following on from deliveries of Leyland Atlanteans, the Fleetline was to become the standard double-decker for Bournemouth during the 1970s, though later examples would be badged as Leyland rather than Daimler Fleetline. NFX 134P was one of eleven to be fitted with convertible open-topped bodies and destined for a long life in Bournemouth, not being finally withdrawn until 2001 and then passing directly to Quantock. It is seen here being repainted in green and cream with the top waiting to be done.

Left

One of thirty Leyland Titan PD2/3 double-deckers with Weymann bodywork new in 1950. They were full fronted and had the Bournemouth speciality of front and rear entrance/exits together with twin stair cases. Designed to allow speedy loading and unloading, the front staircases were later removed and replaced with additional seating. KEL 131 arrived in Somerset in 2006 requiring restoration but was passed on to new owners for this to be undertaken. Note missing lower deck window pans, some repanelling, and the gaffer tape holding in the windscreen. It has also lost the original chrome trim to the radiator and the enamel and chrome town crest.

Above
Fleet number 2534 in original condition in this busy scene at Lower Moseley Street Bus Station in Manchester; a mixture of vehicles from a variety of fleets forms the background. Probably it was a summer Saturday when it was necessary to hire in vehicles to provide the large number of duplicates to clear the crowds. (Ribble Enthusiasts Club Collection)

THE HISTORY

Before the Second World War, Ribble Motor Services of Preston had developed a number of medium distance express routes linking various towns and cities, including seaside resorts, throughout Lancashire and adjoining counties. In the early post-war years, these were proving very popular and hence would require the frequent use of duplicate vehicles. To increase available capacity, A.S. Woodgate, the Ribble chief engineer, developed a design for a double-deck coach body. Production of an initial thirty examples on the Leyland Titan PD1/3 chassis was to be by Burlingham, the coach building firm based in Blackpool who were already a regular supplier of standard double and single-decker service buses.

The result, as will been seen from the photographs, was a full fronted, concealed radiator vehicle with a manually operated jack-knife door and the exterior finished off in a mainly cream livery with various polished metal decorations – so they certainly looked the part, though actual performance would not have been that sparkling from the Leyland E.181 7.4 litre engine. The body was to the traditional lowbridge design with the long bench seat upstairs for four passengers and the sunken gangway on the offside. Upper deck opening roof lights helped brighten the interior; these were protected by metal bars and it has been said that these were fitted following over-exuberant passengers attempting to climb out and get a better view of the Blackpool illuminations!

BUILDERS OF

DOUBLE and SINGLE DECK

PUBLIC SERVICE VEHICLES

and

LUXURY COACHES

H. V. BURLINGHAM LTD.

PRESTON NEW ROAD   BLACKPOOL

Phone: MARTON 251/252/253

Downstairs, the usual longitudinal bench seats over the rear wheel arches were replaced by single forward-facing seats with the remaining space used for luggage storage. Overhead luggage racks were provided on the nearside; the offside was of course occupied by the upstairs sunken gangway. Additional luggage space was also provided in a small and awkward 'boot' under the back platform and accessed from the rear of the coach. The /3 designation in the chassis code indicated that it was designed for 8ft wide bodywork. At this time, 7ft 6in was the standard width for buses and coaches and to use 8ft wide vehicles required specific permission from the Traffic Commissioners. Great play was made of the fact that the extra six inches had been used to provide wider seats, though these were very much of bus, rather than coach, style.

On 24 July 1948, the first new coach entered service on a run from Blackpool to Manchester and the remaining twenty-nine were delivered over the following six months. Registered as BRN 261-BRN 290 and originally given fleet numbers 2519-2547, they would later be renumbered 1201-1230 as part of a scheme allotting blocks of numbers to vehicle types, double deck coaches being allocated the block 1201 to 1300.

A further twenty examples arrived in 1950/51 but this time the bodies were built by

Above
Burlingham were obviously proud of their labours and used an example of the new coaches in their publicity material.

Right
East Lancashire bodied fleet number 1247, DCK 218, with the blinds set for the X50 Manchester to Morecambe, via Preston, service; a run timetabled to take just over 2½ hours. It is probably waiting time to take up service and parked in a side street near Lower Moseley Street Bus Station, Manchester.
(Ribble Enthusiasts Club Collection)

East Lancashire Coachbuilders of Blackburn who had not previously supplied bodies to Ribble other than three examples during the war. They were registered DCK 202-DCK 221 with fleet numbers 1231-1250. Virtually identical to the earlier Burlingham examples, they were of four rather than five window bay construction and had a different folding door and emergency door arrangement. Also featured was a revised radiator grille which was subsequently included on the earlier Burlingham examples; it is understood that this design provided improved engine cooling and certainly looked better. More power was available from the Leyland PD2/3 chassis fitted with the larger 9.8 litre engine.

The origins of the name 'White Ladies' for these vehicles cannot be fully established. The Ribble monthly staff bulletin in the summer of 1948 announcing the original, Burlingham, bodied examples does not mention the name. However, a 1951 edition of the bulletin announcing the East Lancashire examples is headlined 'MORE WHITE LADIES', so there is proof that the name was officially used but there is no evidence of it being used for publicity purposes. Speaking to someone who regularly travelled on them at the time confirmed that the public knew them as White Ladies. The early 1950s would be a time when you didn't really need such things as names, route branding, gimmicks etc to attract passengers; they came anyway. How times change! Obviously the livery had a part to play in the name but Samlesbury Hall, a few miles east of Ribble head office in Preston, is renowned as one of the most haunted locations in Britain. Resident spirits include the legendary White Lady, Dorothy Southworth, who died of a broken heart and has since been seen on many occasions within the Hall and grounds; but there are no reports of her having been seen travelling by bus!

Right
East Lancashire bodied fleet number 1234, DCK 205, standing alone in an empty, wet, desolate Burnley bus station. The blinds are showing service X55, Colne to Blackpool, via Burnley, Blackburn and Lytham St. Annes. (Ribble Enthusiasts Club Collection)

From 1955, the earlier Burlingham examples were downgraded to bus work, with luggage racks removed and livery changed to all over red with cream band. They attracted the very unofficial name of 'Scarlet Women'! All had been withdrawn by 1959 and passed to independent operators for further service before eventually being scrapped.

The later East Lancashire bodied examples were all withdrawn in 1961 and again readily found buyers in the independent sector, ten of the twenty going to Premier Travel of Cambridge to update their double-deck fleet. Apart from the obvious change to their blue and white livery, the main modification made was to increase the lower deck seating capacity by removing the luggage storage over the rear wheel arches and installing additional seats. At this time, Premier Travel tended to replace their service bus fleet in batches and the White Ladies took over from a collection of mainly utility Guy Arabs and later, Bristol K double-deckers. The White Ladies in turn were to be replaced in the early 1970's by AEC Bridgemasters from City of Oxford Motor Services.

Above left
Burlingham bodied 1211, originally 2528, with the updated radiator grille. Comparison with East Lancashire bodied example just visible alongside indicate slight variations in the position of side, head and fog lights. 1211 shows the emergency exit immediately behind the driver's cab door and reference to the picture of 1234 on the previous page shows the exit at the rear of the vehicle. (Ribble Enthusiasts Club Collection)

Left
Fleet number 1217 now down-graded to bus work. Stripped of many of its polished metal mouldings, painted red with just a single cream band and carrying a side advertisement.
(Ribble Enthusiasts Club Collection)

THE SURVIVOR

With the passage of time, only one White Lady was to survive, an East Lancashire bodied example, Ribble Fleet Number 1248 – registration DCK 219. The pictures on this page show it in service with Ribble.

Right
Saturday 4 June 1960 and 1248 is in Lower Moseley Street Bus Station, Manchester, ready for the 1½ hour run on the X53 to Burnley. Obviously a nice day with the windows on both decks open. Both the windows on the driver's cab are open too; it could be hot and noisy enclosed in there with the engine. The crew, who seem to be in no hurry to get away, have open necked shirts but are not wearing summer dust jackets. (John Kaye)

Below left
The year is 1958 and 1248 is in Lancaster Bus Station ready for departure for Blackpool on the X42 service, which would have started its journey in Morecambe. (John Cockshott)

Below right
Here, 1248 is en route from Morecambe to Manchester, with a healthy load of passengers, on the X50 service.
(Ribble Enthusiasts Club Collection)

Following service with Ribble, 1248 was purchased by Reliance Motor Services of Newbury, Berkshire, spending four years with them mainly on contract services taking workers to the Atomic Energy Establishments at Aldermaston and Harwell. In 1966, it joined its comrades at Premier Travel and is understood to have been originally purchased as a source of spare parts. However, it was then considered too good to break and thus prepared for service with fleet number 187, escaping the modifications to the lower deck seating made by Premier Travel to its other examples.

Buses magazine of February 1973 announced that DCK 219 had been sold for preservation; this vehicle was the prime candidate for rescue as it had retained the original lower deck seating layout. It was then to pass through various hands before ending up in Somerset as an unfinished project in 2001. Though much restoration had been done, further work both mechanically and bodily was required to bring 1248 back to original condition. This included having the seats frames renovated and recovered in specially commissioned moquette to the original Ribble specifications; likewise some of the decorative mouldings, including the front bumper, had to be remanufactured.

Following restoration, 1248 made numerous appearances at events all over the country but was later sold on to Brian Souter and now forms part of the Stagecoach heritage collection. Unfortunately, few photographs were taken during restoration and these here and the words in the text do not really do justice to the research, time and money spent on the restoration.

Above left

DCK 211, originally Ribble 1240 and now Premier Travel 137, stands in the depot yard; the blue livery suited the White Ladies well. It will be noted that 137 now carries a Leyland badge above the radiator grille; this is of the style used on the 'Midland Red' style concealed radiators and various heavy lorry models. Alongside is DCK 219, which has lost its front bumper and not yet gained a Leyland badge. (Robin Hannay)

Above right

A lovely sunny day and here DCK 219 is probably at Chrishall depot, to the south of Cambridge, then the main engineering base. The water level is being checked and the filler cap remains to be closed. The flashing indicators would seem to be an 'extra' added by Premier Travel and it will be noted are in a different location to DCK 211. There are also differences in positions of the head and side lights between the two buses. (John Boylett collection)

Right

187 in service with Premier Travel and seen here in Cambridge Drummer Street bus station. There is now a Leyland badge on the front grille but the front chrome bumper is still missing. The vehicle alongside is an ex-Devon General AEC Reliance, and following Premier Travel practice was one of a batch of nine purchased in 1969 to replace ex-London Transport RFs. The Weymann bodies were unusual in having an external, sliding cab door as well as the normal access from inside the saloon. (Philip Hanwell)

Above left and right
The finished article looking resplendent back in the Ribble colour scheme. It is interesting to note that that the moulding around the middle of the vehicle dips down over the top of the offside lower deck windows but not on the nearside. The rear luggage 'boot' door was an upward hinging section incorporating the rear number plate: a small, awkward space which I am sure the conductor did not relish accessing it to stow and later retrieve a passenger's luggage. (Bob Brimley)

THE INSPIRATION

Inspired by DCK 219 and its restoration, Quantock Motors went on to perpetuate the White Lady name and style.

Firstly was the rather unlikely start with a London Routemaster! RM 787 new in 1961, remaining in service with London Transport right through to the 1994 privatisation and passing with the London Central unit to Go-Ahead. During this time, the original AEC engine had been replaced by a Scania unit and the body refurbished, including inward opening hopper windows substituted for the original wind down variety. All the electrics were overhauled, with fluorescent lighting installed and seating and internal trim replaced. Its final years were spent on route 36 Lewisham to Queens Park (though later cut back to New Cross Gate) running from New Cross Garage, finally being withdrawn in January 2005 and passing to Ensign, the dealers, when the route was converted to one person operation with Volvo B7TLs. As with many Routemasters, its registration mark was changed in the months before withdrawal and WLT 787 became 792 UXA. Purchased by Quantock from Ensign in April 2005, RM 787 underwent a transformation to open topper by Cobus, emerging in White Lady inspired livery and sporting the name proudly on the front. In the event, RM 787 did not stay long with Quantock but passed to York Pullman where it was to retain the basic livery but unfortunately lost the White Lady name.

Below
RM 787 following collection from Ensign and taking a break at the M25 Clacket Lane Services on its journey back to Somerset.

Right
Transformation complete and looking much better for it! Despite the destination display it is in action at a Winkleigh open day. (Bob Brimley)

There was then more to follow! In 2005 Quantock had commenced operating the very scenic service 300 along the Somerset and North Devon coast between Minehead and Ilfracombe passing through Porlock, tackling the notorious Porlock Hill and calling at Lynton/Lynmouth and Combe Martin. Again influenced by the White Lady, a brand new partial open top double-decker was purchased. YN55 RDV was a Scania OmniDekka appropriately bodied to special order by East Lancashire Coachbuilders and included seats trimmed in the same moquette as the original Ribble White Ladies. The story of the 300 route and its operation over spectacular and very steep terrain warrants a separate book of its own but with successive cuts in local council support, it was initially cut back to run Minehead to Lynmouth only and finally all subsidies withdrawn. Quantock however continue to run a summer seasonal service using buses from its heritage fleet. YN55 RDV was sold to West Coast Motors, Campbelltown, Scotland and in 2016 was in use on their Glasgow City Sightseeing service.

Right
The two White Ladies together; an East Lancashire Coachbuilders advertisement that appeared in the Bus and Coach Buyer magazine preview edition for the 2006 Coach Rally.

Opposite Page
Above left
YN 55 RDV has just made the descent of Porlock Hill and is picking its way through the streets of the village on the way to Minehead. (Bob Brimley)

Below left
YN 55 RDV and again is negotiating the narrow streets of Porlock village. (Dave Allen)

Right
Publicity material for the 2006 service on the 300 route.

The Way Forward

East Lancs

East Lancashire Coachbuilders Ltd
Lower Philips Road
Whitebirk Industrial Estate
Blackburn
BB1 5UD

www.elcb.co.uk

0044 1254 504150

Weddings

Left and far left
Two of the Quantock Heritage fleet on wedding duties; ex-North Western L5G AJA 132 suitably decorated and ex-Western National Lodekka VDV 752, Admiral Boscawen, in a picturesque setting. On this occasion the crew were invited to join the wedding breakfast; just one of the perks of the job!

One of Quantock Heritage's major aims has always been to make the public in general as aware as possible of the different types of vehicles and their operation experienced in bygone years by previous generations. Particularly during the summer vintage vehicle rally season, it has been policy to present and, when required, operate vehicles at as many rallies and similar events as possible. These include events not only in the south of the country, but also in the north of England. However, travelling long distances from home base in Somerset can be costly, in particular in terms of time and fuel consumption. The average

half-cab single-decker from the 1940s is unlikely to achieve a speed more than forty miles per hour, if that, while average fuel consumption on such a vehicle would – with luck – be around fifteen miles to the gallon of diesel. Once vehicles have been fully restored, it has been possible to make them suitable for operational service by fulfilling specific legal requirements. In particular, this includes appropriate DVSA testing, insurance, and operational licensing. In addition, tachograph equipment recording driver's hours and other information would have to be installed in the cab – a feature certainly not needed when they were first on the road!

By utilising vehicles for private hire work, the ensuing revenue can offset the cost of restoration on further vehicles as well as maintaining the restored fleet. Private hire has included day excursions, business events, school 'proms', sporting events, and other events including, of course, weddings and even funerals. In addition, restored vehicles are occasionally offered for sale. This serves two purposes; it enables individuals and groups who, for whatever reasons, are unable to restore vehicles themselves and, secondly, it can enhance the Quantock Heritage fleet financially in particular in supporting future restorations.

TOWARDS THE END, FOUR TIGER CUBS

For over fifty years, Crossley Motors of Manchester were a significant manufacturer of motor vehicles up to their closure in 1958. During their early years, increasing demands for the wide variety of vehicles they had started to produce resulted in their purchase of a site in Stockport where a factory was built which rapidly became involved in producing vehicles for the First World War, particularly chassis built for the Royal Flying Corps, carrying a mixture of ambulance, light truck, and car bodies. A declining market for their cars in the late 1920s encouraged the company to start the production of bus chassis in 1928. Some years later, large quantities of military vehicles were produced, this time for the Second World War, these being primarily four-wheel drive chassis for use both as tractor units and lorries. The cessation of hostilities resulted in a major increase in the need for new buses, many companies and corporations having suffered losses of vehicles during the war. Crossley won one of the largest bus exports ever, supplying 1,175 vehicles for the Netherlands State Railways bus fleet.

After the First World War Crossley had bought shares in the aircraft manufacturer A.V. Roe Company (Avro's) in the site adjacent to Crossley's in Stockport. They also became involved with the American Willy's Overland Company, but their shares in Avro's had to be sold in 1928 to pay for losses incurred with the latter. After the Second World War, it became evident that the Company could not survive

Above
NDB 356, the Stockport Tiger Cub following restoration and with the Quantock Heritage Fleet.

Left
The aluminium motif also fitted to other Park Royal vehicles, including a preserved ex.-East Yorkshire Motor Services Albion Aberdonian.

on its own and it was taken over by Associated Equipment Company (AEC) in 1948. In turn, AEC became Associated Commercial Vehicles (ACV) and although vehicle production continued in Stockport until 1952, thereafter bus production was under the AEC badge until the factory was closed in 1958.

Stockport Corporation Transport ordered two batches of Crossley bodied buses in 1958 immediately prior to the factory closing. These were ten Leyland Titan PD2/30s and four Leyland Tiger Cubs. These would be the last bodies made by the factory. However, perhaps the more accurate definition of the body maker as far as some of the PD2s should be Crossley/ Stockport Corporation Transport. By this time, staff at the Crossley factory had been reduced, resulting in unsatisfactory delays in completing the order. The Corporation accepted the remaining vehicles in a partly finished state, hired some former Crossley employees who then found the missing parts in the Errwood Park factory and completed the unfinished bodies. The four Stockport Tiger Cubs replaced the ageing fleet of pre-war Leyland TS7s and TS8s, and the Cubs, although bodied by Crossley, show Park Royal influence, Park Royal by that time being part of the ACV group. In particular, the aluminium motif on the front of the Cubs was basically the same as fitted to other Park Royal single-deckers of the period. After various owners in preservation, NDB 356 eventually became part of the Quantock Heritage Fleet.

Above
While still with the Corporation, NDB 356 loads up on a wet afternoon in Mersey Square on the route on which they were primarily used, Stockport's 75, heading for Offerton. (Travel Lens Photographic)

Right
Interior restoration; minor repairs to wheel arch and woodwork, and side panels rubbed down.

EVD 406; FROM BAXTER'S TO WOOD'S

Crossley supplied large quantities of double-deckers in the post war period, including orders from Corporations such as Manchester, Birmingham, Liverpool, Bolton, and of course Stockport, although orders from the latter were as much about supporting local industry as wanting that particular manufacturer's products. Baxter's of Airdrie bought a DD42/7 model in 1949, EVD 406, fitted with a Scottish Commercial body. It was sold to J. Wood & Son, Mirfield, Yorkshire, in 1952. Wood's had run a Crossley Condor six cylinder single deck bus which had proved to be very satisfactory throughout the war years, hence their decision to buy the DD42/7. Serious defects however were found on the body and it was dispatched to Charles H. Roe for a new body to be fitted around 1954. It is likely the order (which would cost £2,043) would have been tacked on to a larger order to Roe's, possibly for Sheffield Corporation. Park Royal had previously acquired a controlling interest in Roe, so both body builders had become part of the ACV Group along with Crossley itself. While with Wood's, EVD 406 ran for some fourteen years on the Mirfield-Dewsbury service, along with J.T. Longstaff and Yorkshire Woollen.

Right
EVD 406 was finally withdrawn by Wood's in 1967. Following withdrawal, it was fully restored by them, including being re-upholstered. It is seen shortly after joining the Quantock Heritage fleet in 2010.

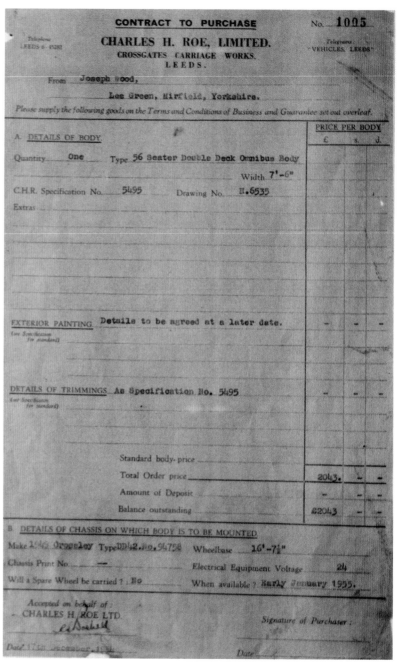

Above
EVD406 while with Baxter's and with its original Scottish Commercial body with which serious defects were found when purchased by Wood's.

Right
Crossley would continue to advertise their products at the 1950 Commercial Motor Show even though (as can be seen at the bottom of the advertisement) now in the ACV Group.

Far right
Joseph Wood's order to Charles H. Roe for the purchase of a new body for EVD 406. Brief and to the point!

Utilising the Old to Create New

CUT AND STRETCH!

As described elsewhere, after the Second World War hostilities had finished, many operators faced problems with ageing and run-down fleets. Orders for new vehicles were slow in being fulfilled with demand in initial years outstripping production. In addition to ordering new, those operators who also chose to re-body pre-war vehicles found body makers facing production problems. This in turn led to a number of smaller body makers increasing their production capacity to try and meet operators' demands, but once operators' fleets had been suitably modernised, many of the smaller body makers would cease to exist.

However, one body builder, J.C. Beadle of Dartford, developed a reputation in the early post-war period in addition to producing conventional bus and coach bodies. They would commence building integrally constructed vehicles for BET companies, but their approach was rather different. A redundant pre-war vehicle would be stripped of its body and then the chassis cut into two sub-frames, front and rear, keeping axles, engines and other relevant units in their original mountings while constructing a new body frame appropriately strengthened to which the sub-frames could be attached. The chassis could be extended to the newly permitted 30ft length allowing more seating capacity. The body design, now 8ft wide and full-fronted, would appear much more modern and stylish than that of a contemporary vehicle with traditional half-cab and exposed radiator. Such attempts to 'modernise' single deck vehicles however would be short lived, as under floor-engined single deck chassis, allowing body builders much more flexibility in body design particularly to the front of vehicles, began

Above
The interior of the ex-East Kent Leyland-Beadle GFN 273 – East Kent vehicles did not carry fleet numbers, being identified by their registration numbers. The quality of finish of the interior is typical of vehicles of the period, and is particularly evocative on GFN 273, being totally original.

to become more common. The appearance of Beadle bodywork would be further enhanced on the front and sides of the vehicles by the use of polished mouldings. This was a feature to be utilised by a number of operators at the time to give their vehicles a more 'contemporary' appearance, including, among others, Ribble, Barton and Birch Brothers, who used polished trim on double–deckers employed particularly on express and long-distance services. Beadle's reputation for building such vehicles was based on experience gained during the Second World War in producing aluminium components for the aircraft industry. Initially produced using Bedford running units, during the early 1950s, full-fronted integrally constructed coaches were built for the BET group utilising pre-war running units from Leyland and AEC chassis. Maidstone & District, East Kent, and Southdown all operated such rebuilds. An East Kent version, GFN 273, dating from 1952 and utilising running units from AJG 30, a 1938 East Kent Leyland TD5 double-decker, joined the Quantock Heritage fleet in 2015. Originally in the care of a group of preservationists in the South-East, since joining Quantock a completely rebuilt engine has been fitted and other minor restoration work carried out. However, the vehicle is basically sound, with a highly original interior.

Beadle became part of the Rootes Group in 1951, particularly promoting the Commer TS3 two stroke diesel engine for integral vehicles (Commer had also become part of the Rootes Group). The Company ceased production in 1958 following reorganisation in the Rootes Group. At that time, integrally constructed vehicles initially received only limited success with bus operators, most continuing to prefer vehicles with separate chassis and bodywork.

Above
Former East Kent Leyland-Beadle GFN 273 shortly after joining the Quantock Heritage fleet. The full-fronted design with the engine to the left of the driver still dictated the entrance to the saloon was behind the front axle and a full width bulkhead would separate the driver from the saloon. Behind the elaborate mouldings on the front of the vehicle would be found the core of the radiator in front of the engine on what was basically a traditional front-engined chassis design.

Left
The use of polished mouldings was not confined to the front of the vehicle, as can be seen above, but would extend all round the windows on both near and off sides.

The 1960s: Four Leylands and an AEC
An East Lancashire Coachbuilders Connection

A LOOK AT FIVE DOUBLE-DECKERS BUILT IN THE 1960s FOR MUNICIPAL OPERATORS, AND ALL WITH BODYWORK DESIGNED, IF NOT BUILT, BY EAST LANCASHIRE COACHBUILDERS LTD.

Above and below
The discreet bodybuilder's plaque usually attached to the panelling around the staircase and is there to greet you as you board, and below the flywheel cover on the front bulkhead.

HISTORY AND BACKGROUND OF EAST LANCASHIRE COACHBUILDERS LTD.

East Lancashire Coachbuilders Ltd. can trace their origins back to the 1930s. Walter Smith had started as a coachbuilder in the Lancashire town of Blackburn, mainly producing bodywork for lorries; however, no work would be turned down and coach bodies for local operators would also be made when requested.

Also around this time, George Danson and Alfred Alcock were working for Massey Bros., the coachbuilders in Wigan. Both gentlemen wished to leave and branch out on their own. They reached an agreement with Walter Smith to establish a new company at his Blackburn premises. East Lancashire Coachbuilders Ltd was registered in October 1934 with Messrs Smith, Danson & Alcock as the only shareholders and directors.

Originally continuing with lorry bodywork, the decision was made in 1937 to make the change to building bus bodies. Orders were soon obtained, mainly from the municipal sector for double-deck bodies. During the Second World War, East Lancashire initially continued to produce bodies to their pre-war styles for both new and secondhand chassis, though shortages of materials meant that interior trim

and finishing were now much more basic. Though not building any bodies to the Ministry of Supply Utility Specifications, East Lancashire became involved in the repair and rebuilding of war damaged buses. War work also involved the assembly of US trucks which had been supplied in kit form. They were unable to fully return to the building and repair of buses until 1944.

An early post-war decision was to standardise on all metal construction for bodywork and although a 'house style' was developed and evolved over the years, they would always build to customers individual requirements whenever necessary. This is demonstrated by the five buses featured here; all have the same basic 1960s style, developed for front-engined chassis but, in addition to the varying colour schemes, all sorts of detail differences and requirements produce quite different looking vehicles.

However, as with most things, nothing is straightforward!! Two of the bodies were in fact not built by East Lancashire at all, even though their name is proudly displayed for all lower deck passengers to see on the flywheel cover on the front bulkhead. These bodies were built by Neepsend Coachworks Ltd. The background to this is that until 1963, all the shares in East

Lancashire Coachbuilders remained with the Smith, Danson and Alcock families but at this time were sold to Cravens Ltd, Darnall, Sheffield, part of the John Brown Group. Cravens had had a long history of tram, railway, bus/trolleybus body building and were interested in re-establishing this. Neepsend Coachworks Ltd was formed as a subsidiary firm of Cravens.

In the beginning, body frames were sent across the Pennines from Blackburn for finishing in Sheffield. Later frames were made in Sheffield though the buses produced were always to East Lancashire designs. The venture was short-lived and production in Sheffield ended in February 1968; labour problems, higher costs and build quality issues were all factors and uncompleted orders passed to Blackburn.

Why the name Neepsend? The factory was near Neepsend Lane to the north west of the city centre. The name is likely derived from an old English word referring to the end of a hill; this makes sense as Neepsend Lane is at the bottom of the valley alongside the River Don.

Just to briefly complete the history of East Lancashire Coachbuilders, they continued as a major player in the bus building market for the rest of the twentieth century, even though ownership changed several times. However, in 2008 a merger with Optare, then based in Leeds, was to eventually mean the end of the East Lancashire Coachbuilders name. Production of all the original East Lancashire bodies ceased by 2011, and the premises in Blackburn closed in 2012.

Right
Though not listed in this advertisement from the Passenger Transport Yearbook *for 1962, all the operators of the buses featured here were also repeat buyers from East Lancashire.*

TENDERS

STOCKPORT CORPORATION TENDERS

TENDERS invited for: (*a*) 15 motor bus chassis with C.I. engines, suitable for double deck bodies, 27ft long and 8ft wide; (*b*) 15 motor bus bodies, metal framed double deck, 27ft long and 8ft wide, mounted on above chassis. Specifications obtainable from General Manager, Transport Dept., Mersey Square, Stockport. Tenders endorsed ''Tender for motor buses'' in plain sealed envelope, to be addressed to The Chairman and Members of Transport Committee, Transport Dept., Mersey Square, Stockport, by August 31, 1965. [1262

Information point:-
The Leyland 0600 engine had been developed after the war and was available for bus use from 1947. It proved to be a very rugged unit and lasted in production until 1972. It takes its designation from its capacity in cubic inches, equivalent to 9.8 litres.

In 1963, the Stockport Transport Committee meeting had authorised the purchase of fifteen new double-deckers every year to ensure the adequate replacement of older Guy and Crossley buses in the fleet. Initially, this was to be the case for the 1965 order; however in the July the General Manager reported on the delayed delivery situation and recommended reissuing a tender for thirty vehicles instead. This was agreed and the resultant batch of buses was again supplied by Leyland and East Lancashire Coachbuilders, who had tendered the lowest prices. The vehicles' specification and appearance were the same as those supplied following the 1963 and 1964 tenders. The Leyland price for chassis was £2,538 10s each and East Lancashire Coachbuilders price for bodies was £3,370 each. Stockport 65 was in fact to be one of fifteen of the order built by Neepsend; it is likely this happened because of the order being increased from fifteen to thirty, which could not be handled at the Blackburn factory.

Left
Stockport Corporation's tender for the original fifteen new buses as advertised in Bus and Coach journal. Compression Ignition (CI) engines are more commonly known as Diesel Engines

Above right
Now with Quantock Stockport 65 is on wedding duty, waiting to take guests to the reception.

Below right
Rear view of 65 at the Quantock depot and being prepared for its next outing.

This gave a total of sixty identical vehicles in the fleet to a very conservative design both mechanically and bodily. Polished aluminium exposed radiators were specified even though deliveries before 1963 had included the more modern looking concealed radiators. The bodies featured inset windows pans rather than the then more common flush, rubber mounted examples and they also had full length metal rain shields over the top of them which again were a rather old-fashioned feature. Coupled with this was the use of wind down windows rather than those with the commonly accepted top slider, contributing further to the very dated appearance. The only concessions to modernity in the interior were the use of Formica laminate lining panels, fluorescent lighting, and translucent roof panels. Mechanically, the continuing use of vacuum brakes was also very old fashioned, with the much more effective air brakes now being widely specified in other fleets. All in all, these buses were about fifteen years out of date when new!

These were to be the last Leyland PD2s to be purchased by the corporation, but at this stage they were still not ready to buy rear-engined double-decker buses and went on to buy the longer Leyland PD3, at 30ft long, first still with open back platform and then later with a front entrance. In fact, Stockport Corporation has the distinction of placing the last open back platform bus in service in the UK, though at this stage, they did also try some dual door Leyland Leopard single-deckers.

In 1967, Stockport Corporation operated a fleet of around 160 buses; a particular feature was a large number of routes run jointly with the adjoining municipal operators of Manchester, Ashton-under-Lyne and Stalybridge, Hyde, Moseley & Dukinfield Transport & Electricity Board as well as company operator North Western Road Car Company whose head office

Above
Stockport Titans in their prime. This picture is taken in Mersey Square, the centre of operations. The Art Deco Plaza Cinema opened in 1932 and on closure it suffered the fate of being used as a bingo hall. However, after work by volunteers and intensive fund-raising, it was completely restored and re-opened as a theatre and cinema in 2009. (David Powell)

Right
In its service life Stockport 65 has proved rather camera shy, so here is 68 standing by boarding hiding the site where the old fire station and tram depot had stood. They had been demolished as part of the Merseyway Precinct shopping development taking place in the 1960's. (Roy Marshall)

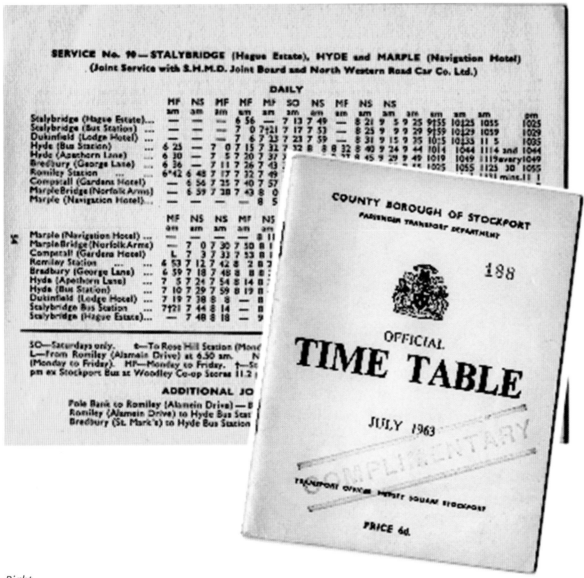

SERVICE No. 19 — STALYBRIDGE (Hague Estate), HYDE and MARPLE (Navigation Hotel)
(Joint Service with S.H.M.D. Joint Board and North Western Road Car Co. Ltd.)

DAILY

		MF	NS	MF	MF	MF	SO	NS	MF	NS	NS				
		am	am	am	am	am	am	am	am	am	am	am	am	am	pm
Stalybridge (Hague Estate)		—	—	—	6 56	—	7 13	7 49	—	8 21	9 5	9 25	9155	1025	1055
Stalybridge (Bus Station)		—	—	—	7 0	7121	7 17	7 53	—	8 25	9 9	9 29	9159	1029	1059
Dukinfield (Lodge Hotel)		—	—	—	7 6	7 23	7 23	7 59	—	8 31	9 15	9 35	10 5	1035	11 5
Hyde (Bus Station)		6 25	—	7 0	7 15	7 31	7 32	8 8	8 32	8 40	7 24	9 44	1014	1044	1114
Hyde (Apethorn Lane)		6 30	—	7 5	7 20	7 37	7 37	—	—	8 45	7 29	2 49	1019	1049	1119
Bredbury (George Lane)		6 36	—	7 11	7 26	7 43	—	—	—	—	—	—	1025	1055	1125
Romiley Station		6*42	6 48	7 17	7 32	7 49	—	—	—	—	—	—	—	—	—
Compstall (Gardens Hotel)		—	6 56	7 25	7 40	7 57	—	—	—	—	—	—	—	—	—
Marple Bridge (Norfolk Arms)		—	6 59	7 28	7 43	8 0	—	—	—	—	—	—	—	—	—
Marple (Navigation Hotel)		—	—	—	—	8 5	—	—	—	—	—	—	—	—	—

		MF	NS	NS	MF	NS
		am	am	am	am	am
Marple (Navigation Hotel)		—	—	—	—	8 11
Marple Bridge (Norfolk Arms)		—	7 0	7 30	7 50	8 1
Compstall (Gardens Hotel)		L	7 3	7 33	7 53	8 1
Romiley Station		4 53	7 12	7 42	8 2	8 7
Bredbury (George Lane)		6 59	7 18	7 48	8 8	8 7
Hyde (Apethorn Lane)		7 5	7 24	7 54	8 14	0
Hyde (Bus Station)		7 10	7 29	7 59	8 19	0
Dukinfield (Lodge Hotel)		7 19	7 38	8 8	—	8
Stalybridge Bus Station		7121	7 44	8 14	—	8
Stalybridge (Hague Estate)		—	7 48	8 18	—	8

SO—Saturdays only.   t—To Rose Hill Station (Mon...
L—From Romiley (Alsmain Drive) at 6.50 am.   N...
(Monday to Friday).   MF—Monday to Friday.   t—S...
pm ex Stockport Bus at Woodley Co-op Stores 11.2 ...

ADDITIONAL JO...

Pole Bank to Romiley (Alsmain Drive) — B...
Romiley (Alsmain Drive) to Hyde Bus Stat...
Bredbury (St. Mark's) to Hyde Bus Station ...

COUNTY BOROUGH OF STOCKPORT
PASSENGER TRANSPORT DEPARTMENT

188

OFFICIAL
TIME TABLE

JULY 1963

COMPLIMENTARY

TRANSPORT OFFICES, DEPOT SQUARE, STOCKPORT

PRICE 6d.

was also in Stockport. The extract on this page from the timetable of the time illustrates the point.

In November 1969, Stockport Corporation Transport Department, along with ten other municipal undertakings covering Manchester and the surrounding area, was absorbed into the South East Lancashire North East Cheshire Passenger Transport Executive (SELNEC PTE). No. 65 became 5865 and was repainted into the new orange and white colour scheme; it is understood that this colour combination was chosen as it had no origin with the absorbed municipal operators and SELNEC could not be accused of any bias. Later reorganisation in 1974 resulted in SELNEC replaced by the Greater Manchester Passenger Transport Executive (GMPTE); an orange based livery was retained. 5865 was to remain in service until January 1981, being used on a farewell tour of Stockport routes as one of the last surviving former Stockport Leyland PD2s. It has been said that in its later years it suffered a lowbridge accident and then considered for conversion to open top, possibly as a replacement for EDB 549 described elsewhere. However, there was union opposition to this and then rather than being withdrawn the upper deck was surprisingly repaired and rebuilt. Given all of this attention,

Right
The 'new order' in SELNEC colours and again 5865, as it has now become, remains camera shy, so here is 5855. SELNEC was initially structured as three divisions; Central, North & South, and these divisions appeared on the sides of the buses with their own specific coloured flashes. 5855 displays the Southern division name with green flashes. The flashes for Central division were blue and for the North, magenta. When the North Western Road Car Company operations in the area were absorbed into SELNEC another division, Cheshire, was formed with brown flashes. (Roy Marshall)

Left

5856 looking as though it has just been freshly repainted into Greater Manchester Transport colours. The destination, Lees, is in the Oldham area so is now operating away from its original home. (Peter Henson)

Below

Former Stockport Leyland Titans galore but still no picture of 5865. A strike by Greater Manchester Transport staff on 19 March 1977 resulted in buses being parked up on land behind Mersey Square in Stockport. This site was later developed to form the present bus station.

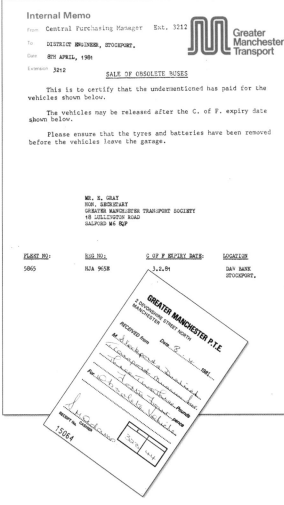

Above

At last an 'in-service' shot of Stockport 65 (GMPTE 5865), taken in Manchester Piccadilly Bus Station not long before final withdrawal on the high frequency 92 service. This began as a joint Manchester/Stockport Corporations tram route. Running from Manchester down the A6 to Stockport and terminating in the southern suburb of Hazel Grove. Today, now numbered 192, it remains a busy service operated by Stagecoach using hybrid double-deckers. (Photo S J Brown, copyright Claire Pendrous)

5865 became an ideal candidate for future preservation and consequently did very little work. None of this has been substantiated but it is a nice story!

Finally, in April 1981, 5865 was purchased for preservation and quickly repainted back into Stockport Corporation red and cream. Finding its way down to Quantock Motor Services in

the 1990s, No. 65 continues to be an extremely reliable vehicle and a very popular choice for wedding hires. Following an initial repaint the only major items of work carried out have been reupholstering the red leather seats and body repairs after some "trouble" with a low bridge. After 20 years in Somerset it has now been treated to another repaint.

Above

Receipts for the original purchase from Greater Manchester Transport of an 'obsolete vehicle'. Note that the buyer will have had to supply their own tyres and batteries; at this time, bus companies often only hired such items.

BLACKBURN CORPORATION TRANSPORT DEPARTMENT

ABV 43B - Fleet No. 43 – Built 1964

Leyland Titan PD2A/24 chassis
  Concealed radiator & fibreglass front
  Leyland 9.8 litre 0600 engine
  Fluid flywheel and Leyland 4 speed
  Pneumocyclic semiautomatic gearbox
  Air brakes
  Body 27 feet long & 8 feet wide

Right
43 in action during a Thomas the Tank Engine event at the West Somerset Railway in Minehead. The destination displayed, HOLE I' TH' WALL, never failed to draw comment; it was a public house built in 1836 and was the birthplace in 1887 of Blackburn Olympic FC, initially a very successful football team though eventually eclipsed by Blackburn Rovers. The pub has now closed and awaiting redevelopment.

Opposite Page
Above: left, middle and right
No. 43 early in its career with Blackburn when it must have been around four years old; the original model Ford Escort following close behind was introduced in the UK at the end of 1967. Route 36 operated from Boulevard, the town centre terminus outside Blackburn Railway Station, to Cherry Tree in the western suburbs, single fare for the whole journey was 6d. From the timetable, it will be seen that route 36 was quite an intensive service from early morning to late at night; Wednesdays & Fridays were market days and required a nine minute frequency to be maintained throughout the afternoon. Heavy printing on thin paper has caused the text on the reverse side to bleed through. (Duncan Holden Collection)

With the East Lancashire Coachbuilders factory in Blackburn it is to be expected that their bodies would be chosen by the local municipal operator, though it was not until 1957 that they became the standard choice. No. 43 was one of 24 similar buses delivered in 1962 and 1964 and, as with other vehicles featured in here, proved to be the last traditional front-engined, open rear platform buses to enter service with Blackburn Corporation; Leyland Atlanteans being delivered in 1968. Following local government reorganisation in 1974 Blackburn Borough Council took over the bus operations of both Blackburn and Darwen Corporations. After withdrawal in early 1981, No. 43 had a spell as a driver trainer, then retained as part of the town's museum collection until 2004 when it was sold for private preservation.

Above
Here seen on wedding duty near Taunton, the destination CHURCH proving particularly appropriate for such occasions. Church is in fact a village just to the west of Accrington.

Information point:-
The Leyland Pneumocyclic gearbox allowed direct selection of the gear ratio required via an air pressure system. Thus, dispensing with the requirement for a clutch pedal.

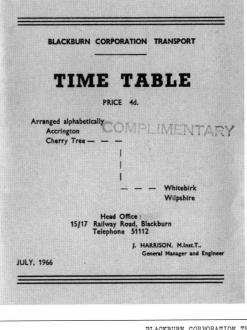

From Boulevard

Monday to Friday
5.15 a.m. and every 9 mins. until 9.01 a.m.
6.19 a.m. and every 9 mins. until 9.01 a.m.
9.15 a.m. and every 15 mins. until 11.30 a.m.
11.43 a.m. and every 9* mins. until 2.16 p.m.
2.30 p.m. and every 15 mins. until 3.45 p.m.
3.55 p.m. and every 9 mins. until 6.46 p.m.
7.00 p.m. and every 15 mins. until 11.00 p.m.
* On Wednesday and Friday, the 9 min. service is maintained throughout the afternoon.

Saturday
5.45 a.m.
6.15 a.m. and every 15 mins. until 10.00 a.m.
10.13 a.m. and every 9 mins. until 7.22 p.m.
7.30 p.m. and every 15 mins. until 9.43 p.m.
9.59 p.m.
10.07 p.m. and every 9 mins. until 11.01 p.m.

Sunday
6.50, 9.25, 9.47, 10.48, 11.42 a.m., 12.55, 1.22 p.m.
1.30 p.m. and every 15 mins. until 10.30 p.m.
Buses pass Witton Park 10 mins. after leaving town.

From Cherry Tree

Monday to Friday
5.28 a.m., 6.05.
6.32 a.m. and every 9 mins. until 9.05 a.m.
9.15 a.m. and every 15 mins. until 11.45 a.m.
11.56 a.m. and every 9* mins. until 2.20 p.m.
2.30 p.m. and every 15 mins. until 3.45 p.m.
3.59 p.m. and every 9 mins. until 6.50 p.m.
7.00 p.m. and every 15 mins. until 11.15 p.m.
* On Wednesday and Friday, the 9 min. service is maintained throughout the afternoon.

Saturday
6.02 a.m.
6.30 a.m. and every 15 mins. until 10.15 a.m.
10.26 a.m. and every 9 mins. until 7.35 p.m.
7.45 p.m. and every 15 mins. until 10.00 p.m.
10.11 p.m. and every 9 mins. until 11.14 p.m.

Sunday
7.00, 9.38, 10.00, 11.01, 11.55 a.m., 1.08, 1.35 p.m.
1.45 p.m. and every 15 mins. until 10.45 p.m.
Buses pass Witton Park 3 mins. after leaving Cherry Tree.

26

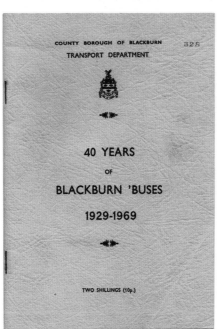

Right
Forty years of municipal bus operation was celebrated in 1969 with this brochure; it is interesting to see the use of the apostrophe in front of the word BUSES; harking back to the time when it was considered an abbreviation for OMNIBUSES.

The contents of the brochure were typed and duplicated and included this rather sparse route map [far right]; buses to Wilpshire, on route 3, would have taken you up Whalley New Road past the East Lancashire works.

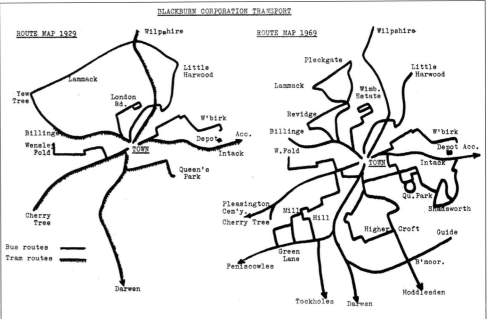

Left and far left
Later, the amount of cream in the livery was increased, and following the amalgamation with Darwen Corporation the colour scheme was changed to include a red roof in recognition of the Darwen colours.
(Mike Rhodes)

Above
Queen Victoria looks down from the left of this shot to survey the goings on in the Boulevard bus station; lots of buses but not too many people. The red bus of Darwen Corporation stands out amongst the Blackburn green. (Duncan Holden Collection)

Above
No. 43 moved south to Somerset in 2012, it was in very good order and soon active in the private hire fleet. It has now found a new life as a mobile bar in Scotland. Nearside lower deck windows have been replaced by serving hatches, new seating and tables installed upstairs along with a sliding roof. Whilst it is always regretted that a bus passes out of preservation, No. 43 has not been modified too much and is certainly very well cared for by its new owners. (Vintage Bus Bar)

EASTBOURNE CORPORATION TRANSPORT DEPARTMENT

BJK 674D – Fleet No. 74 – Built 1966

Leyland Titan PD2A/30 chassis
- Concealed radiator & fibreglass front
- Leyland 9.8 litre 0600 engine
- Four speed synchromesh gearbox
- Vacuum brakes
- Body 27 feet long & 8 feet wide

Above and below
1982 and the new acquisition photographed near the owner's home.

No. 74 was one of a batch of fifteen delivered in 1966-67 and again were to be the last traditional front-engined, rear entrance double-deckers for the Eastbourne municipal fleet; subsequent orders were for rear-engined, dual door single-deckers before further double-deckers were purchased. The Corporation had been a long-standing customer for East Lancashire bodies but the choice of Leyland chassis marked a return to the make after buying AECs for the previous fifteen years. Whilst following the basic East Lancashire body shape, much deeper upper deck windows and consequently shallower roof line was specified. They also incorporated an unusual arrangement of opening windows; a combination of hopper type top vents and half drop panes, all this no doubt to get the most benefit from the sea air and the translucent roof panels also contributed to a light and airy upper deck.

Eastbourne Corporation had never operated trams and 1903 saw the first municipal undertaking to place motor buses in service. Over the ensuing years, they built up a comprehensive network of routes which included open toppers operating along the sea front. Southdown provided the out of town services though, to the annoyance of the Corporation, had the popular service to Beachy Head high up on the top of the chalk cliffs just to the west of Eastbourne. With local government reorganisation in 1974 the undertaking became Eastbourne Borough Council Transport Department and the coat of arms and gold lettering were replaced by a rather bland *EBC* logo. No. 74 was to remain in service until 1979 and after a spell as a driver trainer was finally withdrawn in 1982. Purchased by Steve Morris directly from Eastbourne Borough Council, it was used for the 'fun' part of old bus ownership, being used to get out and actually behind the wheel as a break from the unseen hard work of restoration. No. 74 was eventually sold on and still survives as a 'long term restoration project'.

Above
Here is No. 74 in original livery described as blue and primrose. But as Eastbourne was such a sunny place white roofs were specified to help reflect some of the summer heat. No picture of this era would be complete without a Morris Minor in the background. (Alan Snatt)

Above right
No. 74 in later years; the cream livery with just the one blue band was introduced from 1969 with the EBC logo between decks on the front side panel, and a small town crest is just visible above the driver's cab window. It will be seen that the front number plate is between the upper and lower decks rather than the usual place at the bottom of the radiator grille. Was this an attempt to make for more straightforward accident repair? (Maurice Collignon)

Left
A feature of this particular batch of buses was the concave rear corner panel here seen on sister bus No.80; again, presumably an attempt to reduce damage in vulnerable places but it does look rather strange. One can't imagine Eastbourne buses being subject to more damage than elsewhere. It will also be seen that full use is made of advertising space. (Paul Featherstone)

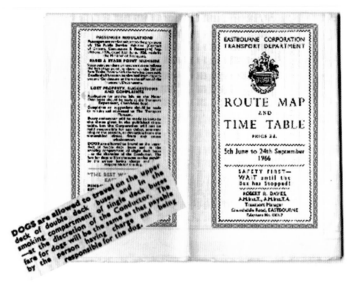

Above
Handy little fold out document containing map, timetable and tourist information produced for the summer season in 1966. There is no mention of the Southdown service to Beachy Head! It is interesting to see that dogs have to pay the same fare as their owner; rather than the more usual separate reduced or half fare.

Above
No. 45 here seen standing outside Taunton railway station on an enthusiasts running day. (Bob Brimley)

Above
The Rossendale fleetname featuring the town coats of arms of Rawtenstall and Haslingden.

ROSSENDALE JOINT TRANSPORT COMMITTEE

XTF 98D – Fleet No. 45 – Built 1966

Leyland Titan PD3/4 chassis
   Exposed radiator
   Leyland 9.8 litre 0600 engine
   Four speed synchromesh gearbox
   Air brakes
   Body 30 feet long & 8 feet wide

Originally new to Haslingden Corporation Transport Department; XTF 98D was their biggest bus yet with seats for seventy-three and their first double-decker with a front entrance. For this honour, the Corporation started their fleet numbering series again and it proudly carried fleet No.1. A similar vehicle, No. 2, was purchased in 1967; though classified as a PD3/14 there was no change to the technical specification, it was just that Leyland had revised their classifications. The Haslingden livery was blue and cream and this was complemented by a blue interior. Haslingden Corporation fleet was small, totalling only fifteen vehicles in 1967, and for some years a general manager had been shared with neighbouring Rawtenstall Corporation Motors. In April 1968, the two undertakings were merged to form the Rossendale Joint Transport Committee with a total fleet of sixty buses. A crimson and cream livery, not unlike Rawtenstall's maroon, was adopted. Haslingden No.1 was duly repainted and renumbered 45 in the combined fleet, as in the accompanying pictures.

Sharing the same manager had of course resulted in a similar vehicle purchasing policy and the two fleets were easily combined. Rawtenstall already had similar Leyland PD3s, though it is interesting to note that some had sliding rather than folding doors. The next purchases were to be single-decker Leyland Leopards. For completeness it should also be noted that the same general manager also looked after the Ramsbottom Urban District Council Transport Department fleet, though in 1969 this became part of the SELNEC PTE.

Above left
Haslingden No. 1 en route to Bacup, about five miles to the east of Haslingden. The name, Bacup, is likely derived from the Old English meaning 'Valley by a ridge'. Concrete bus shelters, with a corrugated roof were once common throughout the country; it looks as though the glazing is still intact with posters attached. (John Walker)

Above right
Here seen in later life as Rossendale No. 45. The location is Burnley Bus Station and the date is 18 January 1978. (Thomas W.W. Knowles)

Left
Haslingden No. 1 nearside view, sitting in the depot with an all Leyland PD2 alongside.
(Roy Marshall)

With local government reorganisation in 1974, the Rawtenstall and Haslingden boroughs were merged to form the Borough of Rossendale, and the Joint Transport Committee became the Rossendale Transport Department.

No.45 is understood to have remained in service until 1982, purchased for preservation, but then stored away for around twenty-five years before becoming part of the Quantock fleet. This was certainly supported by the large amount of dirt and dust that had accumulated in the bus. Externally, some repanelling was required followed by a repaint. Internally, the best of the blue leather upholstered seats were fitted in the lower deck and a new set trimmed in a suitable vinyl installed upstairs, some light fittings replaced and then finished off with a thorough clean. No. 45 was then ready to go back on the road putting in several years work on wedding and other private hires, as well as numerous enthusiast events. It has subsequently moved on to new operators for similar work in Oxfordshire.

Right
Minehead on an enthusiasts' running day; with an appropriate destination on a wet and windy day. Water is a village to the north of Rawtenstall out towards Burnley. Another destination that always caused comment was Cowpe; a hamlet this time to the south east of Rawtenstall, and it is likely the name is derived from Cow Pastures. (Dave Allen)

IPSWICH CORPORATION TRANSPORT DEPARTMENT

DPV 65D - Fleet No. 65 – Built 1966

AEC Regent V 2D2RA chassis

- 2D = standard weight chassis and AEC 9.6 litre AV590 engine
- 2 = Fluid flywheel and AEC 4 speed Monocontrol semiautomatic gearbox
- R = right-hand drive
- A = air brakes
- Body 27 feet long & 8 feet wide.

At this stage AEC chassis designations did not refer to chassis width or length; the option of 7 feet 6 inches wide chassis, and also exposed radiators, had been discontinued in the early 1960's.

Left
Here, No. 65 is seen on duty at Minehead in connection with a Thomas the Tank Engine event organised by the West Somerset Railway. The destination Electric House refers to the Ipswich Corporation Electricity Department offices and showrooms built in the town centre in the 1930s and long used as a terminus for bus services. After various other uses, the building is now the local offices of an estate agent. The adjacent Tower Ramparts Bus Station took over as the town centre terminus.

Below
Looks good from the back as well. The unusual layout of the original green and cream livery is enhanced by the use of red wheels and large 'tramway style' gold, shaded fleet numbers. (Dave Allen)

Ipswich Corporation initially relied on trams and trolleybuses, with the first motor buses not being purchased until 1950. From then the fleet was 100 per cent AEC until the purchase of Leyland Atlanteans in 1968.

Number 65 was the first of a batch of four vehicles that followed from twenty-six similar buses delivered between 1960 and 1963; but just to add variety there had been two Massey bodied examples supplied in 1964. This batch of four were built by Neepsend and proved to be the last traditional front engined, open rear platform buses delivered to Ipswich. Their next buses were AEC Reliance single-deckers with Massey dual door bodywork.

Information point:-
AEC engine designations of this era consisted of a 3 figure number with an A prefix combined with either a 'V' referring to 'vertical', for use in front-engined double-deckers or 'H', for 'horizontal' versions as fitted to underfloor-engined single-deckers. The three-figure number is based on the engine's capacity in cubic inches. Thus the AV590 engine was the vertical version and had a capacity of 9.6 litres. The AEC Monocontrol gearbox allowed direct selection of the gear ratio required via an electrical system, thus dispensing with the requirement for a clutch pedal.

Left
Brand new No. 65 in early February 1966. No fleet name is carried, just the town crest, and the only reference to Ipswich is in the legal lettering. This was common practice with municipal operators at the time; obviously their own livery and the crest was considered sufficient for local citizens to identify 'their' buses. The AEC letters on the radiator grille were a modernising feature of the 1960s but invariably soon disappeared. Again, no picture of this era would be complete without a Morris Minor in the background. (Geoff Mills)

Above
No. 65 parked up in a litter strewn side street (now long gone in town centre redevelopment) which was only used by buses during 1976 when the Tower Ramparts Bus Station was being built. By now it has acquired a much plainer fleet number, but as predicted, the AEC lettering from the radiator grille has gone. (Stuart Ray)

Left
A foul day outside the depot in Constantine Road. The back end of one of the AEC Reliances with Massey body can just be seen on the left of the picture. (Philip Hanwell)

Above left
Regents galore at the Tower Ramparts bus station. Electric House is close by. (Keith Halton)

Above right
No. 65 returning to town on its very last run in service on 2 August 1986. The homemade board on the radiator grille proclaiming REGENT V FAREWELL. Note the revised livery adopted with the 1974 reorganisation and it is now seen necessary to put an actual fleet name on the side of the bus. Fleet numbers are a little more ornate again. (Stuart Ray)

Right
Extract from Buses *magazine July 1986. As with the Stockport purchase, the tyres were extra; again such items were not owned but hired.*

With local government reorganisation in 1974 the undertaking became Ipswich Borough Transport and No. 65 remained with them and by 1986 was one of their last two crew operated buses. At the time *Buses* magazine noted that AEC Regent V operation, with the ongoing availability of a conductor, would continue to the August of that year. Ipswich Borough obviously wanted No. 65 to go to a good home and it was advertised in *Buses* magazine, July 1986. Steve Morris spotted the advert and bought the bus, though at the time his purchase caused some confusion in reporting it in the magazine. Firstly, his namesake, the then editor, had to advise that it was not him who had bought No. 65 and then a reference to a connection with Liebherr, the large, multinational engineering firm appeared. Steve Morris (the purchaser) worked for Liebherr and though a private purchase, correspondence had been on company headed note paper!

No. 65 was to become a long term member of the heritage fleet and over the years treated to a return to the more attractive original livery, new upholstery and some work on the engine. It has now moved to new owners in East Anglia so is closer to its original home.

(Pictures: Maurice Collignon Dave Allen, Ken Jones & the author)

There we have it, five buses of a similar age all with bodywork to the same basic style from one manufacturer but all looking different! Exposed and concealed radiators, numbers and type of opening windows, front and rear entrances, fixed and opening cab windows, sliding or hinged cab doors all to the operators individual requirements; coupled with some very traditional liveries, lettering styles and destination layouts developed over the years. The same also goes for the interior colours, fixtures and fittings.

Many municipal operators were very cautious in their vehicle purchasing, no doubt not wishing to risk their rate-paying residents' money on what were considered new-fangled products and sticking to what they knew. Though all the buses considered here were certainly very conservative buys, they marked the end of the old order and in most cases these were to be the last traditional front-engined double-deckers to be bought by the municipalities concerned. It is interesting to

see that subsequent purchases included large capacity single-deckers suitable for one person operation which were then seen as the future. Only Stockport went on to take a further number of Leyland Titan PDs but they were later to order rear-engined double-deckers in the form of Bristol VRs, though these were destroyed by fire at East Lancashire Coachbuilders and if they had survived would not have been delivered until after the Stockport Corporation fleet had been absorbed into SELNEC.

These actual vehicles have survived, and we know that Leyland and East Lancashire unfortunately did not, so what happened to the operators in the later 1980s after 'our' buses were withdrawn? This was a period of upheaval resulting from political changes culminating in the 1985 Transport Act that not only deregulated local bus services, and thus allowed them to be opened up to competition, it also required that local authorities operate their buses at arm's length

as limited companies. In 2007, the Blackburn company was purchased by the French group Transdev and it was announced early in 2018 that they had also agreed a deal to acquire the Rossendale operation. In 2008, Stagecoach bought the Eastbourne business to add to their former Southdown interests in the south of England. As noted earlier, Stockport had been absorbed into SELNEC and subsequently into Greater Manchester Transport. From the 1985 Transport Act, Greater Manchester Transport Ltd was formed, though later government pressure forced the division of this into two separate companies, North and South, and their ultimate sale. Employee-owned GMB South Ltd was formed in 1993 with the head office in Stockport; though in 1996, Stagecoach Holdings purchased the company and today continues to provide most of the services in the Stockport area.

Therefore, only Ipswich remains as a company still owned solely by the local council.

BARTON
ROUTES

----- EXPRESS SERVICES
——— BUS SERVICES

TELEPHONE
BEESTON
56261

BARTON
TRANSPORT LIMITED

HEAD OFFICE
CHILWELL
NOTTS.

Barton grew to be one of the largest independent operators in the country. Based in Chilwell, just to the south west of Nottingham, they developed a network of urban and country services throughout the area indicated in the map taken from the ABC Coach guide of 1954. Later acquisitions established a presence further east and south in the Stamford and Peterborough areas and an extensive network of express services throughout the country was also developed.

Until the 1930s, double-deckers did not feature very much in the fleet but initial deliveries came just before the war. Many vehicles from the single-deck fleet were requisitioned by the War Department and this led to a severe shortage of buses to cope with the increased demand for the transport of war workers. This was initially overcome by acquiring a quantity of elderly, second-hand Leyland Titan double-deckers from across the country; their chassis were sound but all were rebodied with Duple double-deck bodies. Later arrivals of wartime, utility Guy Arabs established double-deckers as a significant part of the Barton fleet.

The double-deckers described here all represent aspects of the rich and varied fleet amassed by Barton from the 1940s through to the 1960s and made the company a Mecca for the enthusiast who wanted a bit of variety!

JNN 384 – Fleet Number 467
Built 1947

Leyland Titan PD1 chassis
  Leyland 7.4 litre E181 engine
  Four speed non-synchromesh gearbox
  Vacuum brakes

Duple of Hendon body
  Lowbridge
  26 feet long, 7 feet 6 inches wide
  Forward entrance
  Seating 29 upstairs & 26 down

Before the war, Barton had always favoured Leyland chassis and Duple bodywork for its new vehicles and this combination continued into the 1940s with an order for forty new double-deckers which were delivered between 1947 and 1949. 467 was an early arrival, being delivered in December 1947.

Barton had always had an individualistic approach to vehicle design/appearance and wherever possible ensured that internally they were finished to a high standard of comfort, even for buses used on normal stage services. These forty double-deckers were certainly no exception to this as the following pictures show.

The overall design was a development of that produced for the double-deckers delivered just before the war. The forward entrance with platform doors was not common but had appealed to some operators in the 1930s, though was not followed up after the war when it was more a question of take whatever was available. It is interesting to note that the company operators in the Nottingham area, Trent and Midland General, had favoured the forward entrance in the 1930s and Barton had acquired an example with this layout with the takeover of a local operator.

Above
An unidentified example of the forty new double-deckers in what is likely to be an official photograph taken when new. Note the unusual position of the entrance with the double doors sliding inside the body. The stairs led straight up across the front bulkhead to the upper deck sunken gangway. Notice the rather formidable step up to get inside in the first place.

Below
To complement the extensive use of polished metal trim the prominent fleet name was produced in a similar fashion.

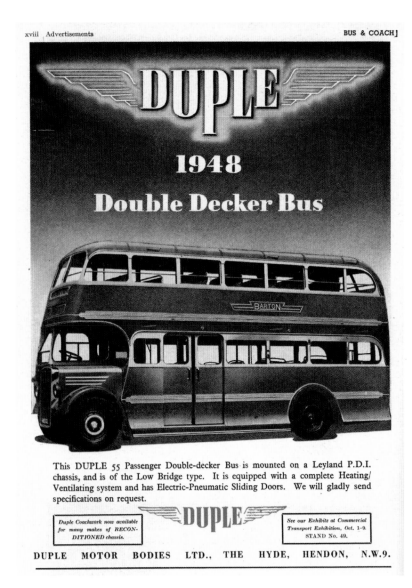

DUPLE

1948

Double Decker Bus

BARTON

This DUPLE 55 Passenger Double-decker Bus is mounted on a Leyland P.D.I. chassis, and is of the Low Bridge type. It is equipped with a complete Heating/ Ventilating system and has Electric-Pneumatic Sliding Doors. We will gladly send specifications on request.

Duple Coachwork now available for many makes of RECON-DITIONED chassis.

DUPLE

See our Exhibits at Commercial Transport Exhibition, Oct. 1–9. STAND No. 49.

DUPLE MOTOR BODIES LTD., THE HYDE, HENDON, N.W.9.

Above
Mount Street, Nottingham in October 1971. Fleet numbers 509 & 453 side by side. Spot the various differences: colour scheme, fleet names, number plate location, polished metal trim.

Left
Duple were justifiably proud of their creation and it featured in this advertisement that appeared in the October 1948 edition of the journal Bus and Coach, self-styled 'The Operators' Journal', which coincided with the 14th International Commercial Motor Transport Exhibition at Earls Court, London. Duple were mainly known for their single-deck coachwork and therefore this was a rather strange choice for their advertisement. There were no orders from other operators for this style of double-decker; the few that were built were to the 'standard' rear platform layout and certainly with much less ornamentation.

Extensive rebuilding of these buses in the late 1950s had retained the main appearance of the Duple body but created a fascinating range of detail differences both externally and internally. Most were to be very long lived, with the final examples remaining in service until 1973. One of the last in service, 467, was not finally withdrawn until March 1973, then being acquired for preservation.

467 subsequently passed through the hands of several owners and arrived with Quantock in 2003 in a very neglected condition. It has now been the subject of a long and extensive restoration as evidenced by the pictures which follow, back to the condition it would likely have been following refurbishment in the late 1950s.

Above
Chilwell Garage, October 1971 and 516 is now in use as a driver trainer. Note the modification to the nearside bulkhead window to enable the instructor to communicate with the trainee. The panel on the side advertises the Barton HGV and PSV Driving school and notes that HP (Hire Purchase) Terms are available to pay for your training. Not the easiest vehicle on which to learn to drive !

Above and below
467 resting between duties at Stamford Garage in June 1971. The panels either side of the destination blinds are advertising Rippin Bangs; not a dodgy nightclub or a predecessor of the household cleaner Cillit Bang but a firm of local estate agents! (Maurice Collignon)

Left
467 as it arrived in Somerset and not really betraying some of the problems that lay beneath the surface.

THE RESTORATION BEGINS...

Left, above and right
The body was stripped right down to allow extensive repair and replacement where necessary of the wooden framework. All probably a bit like Barton had done in the late 1950s. (Bob Brimley & Dave Allen)

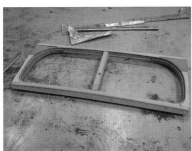

Left and far left
Some parts required complete reconstruction. Here are newly made driver's cab door and upper deck emergency exit. (Scott Payne)

BEFORE AND AFTER...

In all a very complicated vehicle, they must have been extremely labour intensive when built – perhaps a reaction to the very basic utility vehicles of only a few years before. The number of screws just to hold on the exterior polished metal mouldings doesn't bear thinking about.

Above left and right
Major mechanical work was required. Here is the engine out of the bus undergoing testing after a complete rebuild, then painted, reinstalled and looking brand new. (Scott Payne & Dave Allen)

Left
The interior was gutted to give access to the body frame and allow the complete renewal of the electric wiring. Ceilings and sides were completely relined, new wooden flooring and linoleum laid and the large amount of varnished wood trim was either renovated or replaced. Grab rails on the seat backs were re-chromed and the seats re-trimmed with the especially commissioned correct pattern of moquette. Light fittings, ventilator covers, bell pushes, hand rails and other interior metal fittings were all refurbished. In the end this has certainly recreated the cosy style and comfort from a bygone era. (Ken Jones & Dave Allen)

Far Left
The first public appearance for a long time, before all work was finally completed, was back at Barton's Chilwell headquarters on what would have been the 150th birthday of the founder of the company, Thomas Henry Barton: Sunday 25 September 2016. This was likely the last opportunity to visit as the site is now due for redevelopment.

Left and below
Who said the back end of a bus was ugly, surely one cannot fail to see the beauty of such a back end!?! Comparison with the original condition [bottom right] shows that all that rebuilding work was certainly worth it. The illuminated Barton signs above the front & rear destinations were painstakingly recreated by hand.

Below left
The finished article! Carrying passengers for this first time in over 30 years at the New Year's Running Day in Coventry, 2 January 2017. Much head scratching was involved in understanding how the vacuum operated sliding doors worked and then getting them to function. The mechanism for the drop down windows was complex – a lot of wires, springs, catches and pulleys. (Ken Jones)

WAL 782 – Fleet Number 782

Leyland Tiger PS1 chassis, built 1948
  Leyland 7.4 litre E181 engine
  Four speed non-synchromesh gearbox
  Vacuum brakes

Willowbrook of Loughborough body, built 1957
  Lowbridge
  27 feet long, 8 feet wide
  Rear entrance with platform doors
  Seating 31 upstairs & 30 down

Right
Chilwell headquarters in October 1971 and 782 with a few more years in service ahead. Advertisements for the extensive series of Barton express services were a common feature on the sides of the buses. Note how the wheels are set well inside the bodywork, this is the result of an 8ft wide body being fitted on to a 7ft 6in wide chassis; the same also applies to the fuel filler cap. (Dave Allen)

In the early 1950s and following on from the 40 Duple bodied Leyland PD1s, Barton's double-deck requirements were largely met by extensive second-hand purchases, pre-war Leyland Titans figuring very strongly here. Many pre-war and later post-war Leyland Titans were also acquired just for their chassis, which were then cut, lengthened and rebodied as 30ft long single-deckers. Attention was then turned to creating new double-deckers using second-hand chassis. With the introduction of the single deck underfloor-engined chassis and the lighter weight Bedford SB, all with full fronted bodywork to new, modern designs, the front-engined chassis with half-cab coachwork had rapidly become viewed by the travelling public as old fashioned. As operators updated their fleets, there were

some good second-hand purchases available. With their extensive fleet and knowledge of Leyland PD1s and single-deck equivalent the Leyland Tiger PS1, Barton acquired a number of second-hand Leyland Tiger PS1s to supplement some of their own to form the basis of new double-deckers.

782 is an example of one of these, the basis being a Leyland Tiger PS1 with Santus, of Wigan, thirty-three seat coach body supplied new to W.H. Knowles of Bolton, registered CWH 262 in 1948 and subsequently passing through the hands of various owners before acquisition by Barton. The body was discarded, and the chassis despatched to Willowbrook at Loughborough for its new

double-deck body. The chassis designation PS1/B, was adopted to identify the Barton 'input'. 782 entered service in March 1957 and was finally withdrawn in April 1974. It saw further service with J.F & M. Williams of Llangollen, T. Hollis of Queensferry and Cross Roads Travel Ltd of Warrington before being originally secured for preservation in 1978. Acquired in very sound condition by Quantock in 2008, it is now back in the Nottingham area for continued preservation.

Further rebuilds on PS1 chassis were to follow and these included full front, forward entrance bodies by Northern Counties of Wigan. In certain cases, chassis were lengthened to accept 30ft long bodies.

Above left
782, still looking quite smart, outside Ilkeston Garage in February 1965. (Maurice Collignon)

Above right
By April 1974 it was withdrawn and parked at the back of the Chilwell headquarters looking a bit dejected. Notice the different positions of the PARCELS CARRIED notice on the front; these signs were hinged along the top and could thus be raised or lowered to regulate the cooling provided by the radiator. (Maurice Collignon)

Left
Not CWH 262, for which a picture cannot be traced, but a Leyland PS1, CJT 820, with typical Santus body of the period and likely to have been similar, if not identical, to CWH 262. Here it is in service with Bere Regis & District in Dorset. Santus bodywork was not renowned for its longevity with the very curvaceous design and the four bay construction putting great stresses on the wooden framework. The company, like many others, had flourished with the high demand for new coaches after the Second World War but had ceased body building by September 1953. (British Commercial Vehicle Museum)

Above left and right
782 now in preservation and looking very smart on an enthusiasts' running day. Note the unusual treatment of the upper deck, rearmost side windows; two small ones rather than one to cover the platform/stairs area. (Bob Brimley)

Left
1976 and in service with Hollis of Queensferry in North Wales. It must be said that the livery is not as flattering as the Barton version. (Geoffrey Morant)

Below
The Barton flag was adopted in the 1950s and gradually replaced the earlier more ornamental fleet name.

851 FNN – Fleet Number 851
Built 1960

AEC Regent V 2D3RA chassis
  **2D = standard weight chassis AEC 9.6
    litre AV590 engine**
  3 = 4 speed synchromesh gearbox
  R = right-hand drive
  A = air brakes

Northern Counties of Wigan body
  Lowbridge
  30 feet long, 8 feet wide
  Full front, forward entrance
  Seating 37 upstairs & 33 down

Less in the limelight than the Dennis Loline exhibited at Earls Court last September, Barton's five recent A.E.C. Regent Mark V models with Northern Counties bodywork of similar style share an appearance which seems more in keeping with the 'sixties than the austere-looking vehicles being placed in service by some operators. This is No. 851, seen in Derby.

(T. G. Walker)

Above
Buses Illustrated, *January 1961.*

As already mentioned, throughout the 1950s Barton had mainly relied on second-hand purchases and the rebuilt/rebodied Leyland PS1 single-deckers with very few complete, brand new double-deckers entering the fleet. However, in 1960, a batch of five new AEC Regents, fleet numbers 850 to 854 (850 to 854 FNN) arrived. Following on from the latest re-builds on Leyland PS1 chassis, they were also 30ft long, with full fronts and forward entrances but now featuring wraparound windscreens and front upper deck windows. Overall this produced a very stylish vehicle at a time when the new generation of rear-engined buses were very much boxes on wheels. This was recognised in the caption to the picture in *Buses Illustrated* magazine of January 1961, but also noting that these new AECs were rather overshadowed by the ultra lowheight Dennis Loline, fleet number 865, which carried a very similar body. When delivered, this batch of buses were fitted with the Cave-Browne-Cave heating/cooling system with grilles between decks either side of the destination screens. As found by other operators, this system proved troublesome and was removed, the grilles panelled over and a conventional radiator in front of the engine installed. A further batch of six similar buses, fleet numbers 957-962 (957-962 PRR) were delivered in 1963 and had conventional radiators and heating systems from the start.

Left
851 in original condition in a very wet Derby bus station.
(Maurice Collignon)

Below left
851 again in Derby bus station but on a much nicer day. Note the Cave-Browne-Cave grilles either side of the destination have been removed and a hole cut above the AEC grille to accommodate a radiator filler cap. The 5 series of routes between Nottingham and Derby were Barton's main services and invariably worked by the latest vehicles.

The rather basic Guardian Journal advertisement was very common on Barton buses and refers to the city's daily morning paper; formed by a merger of the Nottingham Guardian and the Nottingham Journal in 1953 and lasting until 1973 when it was discontinued following industrial action. (Geoffrey Morant)

Below right
Derby bus station yet again, but this time 851 is in its final role as a driver trainer. Communication between instructor and trainee would have been easy with the wide open bulkhead.
(Philip Hanwell)

Right
Bruised, battered and rather shabby, 851 as originally acquired. A draughty drive for someone with the nearside front windscreen missing. The between decks panel advertises 'Barton's Road Cruise Holidays, Private Hire, Tours & Excursions', and with Cave-Browne-Cave grilles removed.

Information point:-
The Cave-Browne-Cave heating/cooling system was developed by Wing Commander Thomas Cave-Browne-Cave while he was Professor of Engineering at Southampton University. It was a combined engine cooling/vehicle heating & ventilation system which replaced the conventional engine radiator with two grilles above the driver's cab, usually either side of the destination box, to provide maximum air flow. Flaps could divert warm, but fresh, air to heat the bus interior in cold weather or out of the bus in warm weather. Problems arose with air locks in the system and engine cooling could be inadequate if the air flow was reduced under conditions such as protracted periods of slow speed; the result then was that the system would boil over.

851 was to remain in service until 1973 and then used for a period as a driver trainer. Subsequently retained by the company for their 'museum' collection, it however saw little use and had been stored. Though basically sound when acquired in 2007, it was rather shabby as the picture shows. A complete re-paint and reupholster was required, together with a full service mechanically. However there was one major replacement needed; the nearside wraparound windscreen was missing. Not available off the shelf, a wooden pattern had to be made and supplied to the glaziers, and after several attempts they came up with the goods – all in all, a very expensive exercise for everyone concerned. After several years of activity on the enthusiast circuit, with appearances all over the country, 851 has now passed to a new owner for on-going preservation closer to its Nottingham home.

Above

851 now looking particularly smart in front of the impressive, gothic-inspired buildings of Taunton School. Dare it be said that the Northern Counties body looks much sleeker than that being produced by the same concern at the time for the Southdown Queen Marys? Shipstones Ales, a local Nottingham brewery again often advertised on Barton buses. Taken over by the 'big boys' in 1978, brewing ended in 1990 but the name has been resurrected by a private company and brewing recommenced. (Dave Allen)

Right

The Robin Hood name and image were added after the takeover of the firm in 1962, the Hall Bro's name being included with the purchase of this South Shields coach firm in 1967.

Above
Looks good from the back as well, featuring another advertisement for Barton's Express Services.

Above right
Lower deck looking towards the rear.

Right
Upper deck looking forward.

A mixture of old and new styles on the inside. Grey Formica panels and lots of cream paint contrast with the Art Deco seat moquette and the exposed, filament light bulbs at a time when fluorescent tubes were becoming available.

The upper deck sunken gangway and its intrusion into the lower deck can be seen. On the upper deck, the circular object on the front of the gangway is a Clayton Heater, which would have been fitted when the Cave-Browne-Cave system was removed. Basically, these heaters were plumbed into the engine cooling water system and an electric motor fitted with a large propeller would blow out air warmed by the pipes – at least that was the theory!

In the lower deck view, a cream box can be seen at the rear on the emergency exit door. This contained a First Aid box. Attention was drawn to this by the sign on the outside just below the emergency door window.

BRM 596 – Fleet Number 816

Leyland Titan TD4 chassis, built 1936
  Leyland 8.6 litre engine
  Four speed non-synchromesh gearbox
  Vacuum brakes

Eastern Coach Works of Lowestoft body
  Built 1949
  Lowbridge
  26 feet long, 7 feet 6 inches wide
  Rear entrance
  Seating 27 upstairs & 26 down

This is but one example of the many second-hand purchases made by Barton in the 1950's; and along with a further TD4 and 2 TD5's from the same source were the last second-hand pre-war purchases made by Barton. At this time, post-war Leyland Titan PD1s were being acquired from a variety of operators.

BRM 596 was originally Cumberland Motor Services fleet number 132 and fitted with a Massey, of Wigan, lowbridge body; being rebodied in 1949 with a standard Tilling style ECW body and renumbered 291. After a further ten years' service with Cumberland, it passed to Barton in 1959, who then ran it for a further five years, eventually being withdrawn in January 1965. It was then secured for preservation, firstly in Barton colours but reverted to Cumberland livery in 1973. Initially active on the rally circuit and enthusiast trips; it was to pass through various owners until arriving with Quantock in a partially dismantled state and with engine problems. Work on rebuilding an engine for it is in hand and the body restoration is now starting to return it to its former glory. Will it emerge as Cumberland 291 or Barton 816? We will have to wait and see!

Above
A busy scene in Mount Street, Nottingham, bus station with a very smart looking BRM 596 to the fore. In the background, a varied collection of Barton double-deckers, and crews are in animated discussion. The two gents queuing patiently are wearing their best suits but one has his mac in hand; you never know if it might rain.
(John Cockshott)

Right
An official shot of DAO 50 when new; a slightly newer Leyland TD5 but with the same style of original Massey body fitted to BRM 596. DAO 51 would be one of the Cumberland TD5s purchased by Barton.
(Omnibus Society Collection)

THE CUMBERLAND YEARS

Left
BRM 596 in the early years of the war in Keswick bus station awaiting departure for Whitehaven. The headlights have masks fitted as part of blackout restrictions and the front mudguard edges have been painted white to try and help pedestrians pick out a darkened vehicle approaching at night. I'm sure Storms Refreshment Rooms would have provided a good cup of tea to keep spirits up in those difficult times. (S.L. Poole)

Below left
Here, in August 1954, BRM 596 is sporting its new ECW body and parked up outside the rear entrance to Workington bus station prior to a spell on the Town Service; you would need to be a local to know where it actually went. Workington bus station was opened in 1926 and was the first purpose built, covered facility in England. Small, wartime headlights are fitted. (John Cockshott Archive)

Below right
BRM 596 now withdrawn by Cumberland Motor Services. It is likely that this picture was taken at Barton's premises, with one of the three other Leylands from the same source, awaiting attention in the workshops and preparation for further service. The small wartime headlights would be replaced as seen in the picture on the previous page. (Gerald Walker collection)

Left
End of the road with Barton; February 1965 and BRM 596 is parked up out of service at Chilwell. 'NOT LICENCED' is stencilled on the windscreen and closer inspection with a magnifying glass shows 'DRAINED OFF' just above.
(Maurice Collignon)

Right
BRM 596, now in preservation, is parked outside the Wolverhampton Corporation Cleveland Road depot. The date is 5 March 1967, the last day of Wolverhampton trolleybuses operation, and a group of enthusiasts have been brought along to pay their respects.
(Maurice Collignon)

LIFE AFTER BARTON

Left
BRM 596 as initially restored back to Cumberland Motor Services colours and involved in some filming at Whitehaven to create this very atmospheric shot. (Harry Postlethwaite)

Right
The current state of BRM 596 as it starts its latest restoration. Whilst looking complete, the whole of the interior is stripped out revealing that attention is required to the wooden body framing and the staircase. All the seats and various fitting such as hand rails, wooden window cappings and trim are piled up on the lower deck and will need a good sorting out to ascertain what is there and what is missing.
(Bob Brimley)

Leyland Titan PD2/12 chassis
Leyland 9.8 litre 0600 engine
Four speed synchromesh gearbox
Vacuum brakes

Leyland body
Highbridge
27 feet long, 8 feet wide
Rear entrance
Seating 31 upstairs & 26 down

Right
The year is 1959 with RTC 822 hard at work in its home town and pursuing a rather battered Ford van. (Geoffrey Morant)

The final vehicle in this chapter never ran for Barton but earns a place here as it certainly embodies the spirit of Barton and actually includes a physical bit as well.

It was an all Leyland production and with fleet number 18, was one of three similar buses supplied to Rawtenstall Corporation in 1953. It was then to give twenty-one years' service in this Lancashire town before providing transport for Bingo players in the Motherwell and Hamilton area, to the south east of Glasgow, before being acquired for preservation. Like several of the vehicle featured, after initial restoration and activity on the rally scene, including a spell back with its original

municipal owners, it went into hibernation prior to acquisition by Quantock.

With restoration started it was found that the whole of the rear half of the chassis was rotten and the complex job of replacement was required. Consequently the lower part of the body needed to be stripped to its bare frame with all the fittings, seats and floor removed. A replacement section from a donor chassis was inserted, and the body reassembled with the framework repaired, re-panelled and a new floor laid. It was also found necessary to have a new set of lower deck window pans manufactured and all this finished off with the seats being reupholstered. So here was the spirit of Barton who were past masters at cutting,

lengthening and replacing bits of chassis; especially when they belonged to a Leyland. And the physical part? The donor chassis was a Barton vehicle!

RAL 334, Barton fleet number 732, was one of 2 all Leyland PD2/12's purchased in 1954 and one of the very few complete new double-deckers purchased new in the 1950's; so of the same age and specification as Rawtenstall 18. Withdrawn by Barton in April 1974 732 became a playbus in Kent until replaced by an ex London Transport DMS. By the time it arrived in Somerset it was just a chassis/cab and fit only for spares; it had been re-registered APR 167A and it is understood that its original plate, RAL 334, found its way on to a Bentley Continental car.

Above
732 resting between duties inside Chilwell Garage. The later addition of platform doors can be seen.

Above right
Looking as though it has seen better days, Barton 732 is parked up on the open ground behind the Chilwell headquarters. The driver's opening windscreen has a replacement rubber seal, no doubt in an attempt to stop leaks. The Home Ales advertisements on the front were to be found on many Barton double-deckers. Home Ales, founded in 1875, was a Nottingham brewer and remained an independent, family concern until sale to the large Scottish & Newcastle organisation in 1986. Subsequently, the brewery was closed and the brand name phased out. Recently, the name has been resurrected by an independent brewer. (Philip Hanwell)

Then finally just to make things more exciting RTC 822 has not been presented in Rawtenstall colours but repainted in the maroon, black and cream livery of Scout Motor Services Preston; a long-lost independent operator who was taken over by Ribble in 1962. Scout had purchased a Leyland demonstrator, STC 887, of the same vintage and specification as RTC 822. Though it is interesting to note that various reference works refer to STC 887 as a PD2/20 which would indicate a concealed radiator version; was it used by Leyland as a prototype and then converted back to exposed radiator? There are always additional questions!

Bottom right
All that remained of Barton 732 when it arrived in Somerset.

Above
Scout STC887 bouncing over the cobbles in Preston in 1958. A full load on what must have been a warm day as all the windows are open. Note the grinning girl complete with straw boater on the upper deck; had the schools just come out? Rear platform doors can just be seen; these were later addition by Scout, just as Barton had added a similar luxury to their 732.
(John Cockshott)

Above right and right
The lower picture shows RTC 822 resplendent in its new colours on its first public outing at the 2016 Taunton Vintage Bus Day. In the upper picture it is waiting to transport a wedding party to the church. (Ken Jones)

The advertisements are examples of those carried by Scout buses in the 1950's. That on the offside is pretty straight forward and to the point. Red Rose Stout was a product of Groves & Whitnall at their brewery in Regent Street, Salford. They were taken over by Greenall Whitley, who are now no longer involved in actual brewing. It will be seen that Scout STC 887 carries the fleet number 20. RTC 822 has retained its Rawtenstall number, 18, as this is still proudly displayed on the interior bulkhead.

FROM TILLING TO BRISTOLS

Operators purchasing policy was often heavily influenced (and sometimes dictated) by decisions not made by the managerial or engineering staff but by the holding company and other factors, particularly during specific ownership regimes and eras. This was certainly true for long periods of time in the history of Stockport based North Western Road Car Company (their vehicles were always referred to as Cars). Why this occurred is a direct result of the history of the Company itself. In 1913, the British Automobile Traction Company (BAT), a subsidiary of the British Electric Traction Company (BET), realising there was little or no public transport in the rural areas of Cheshire, started to operate out of the Cheshire town of Macclesfield. Operating under the fleet name 'British', considerable expansion took place over the next ten years and a core of routes was established. This expansion necessitated developments both in terms of operational organisation and capital. Thomas Tilling, a holding company with considerable transport interests, had already acquired a large holding in BAT. This resulted in 1923 in the formation of a new Company, the North Western Road Car Company, with Tilling and BAT each holding 50 per cent of the capital. Tilling (under the name Tilling-Stevens) had started to produce and use vehicles which were powered by a petrol-electric system, thus preceding the dual fuel systems which have become common

Above left
British Automobile Traction Company issued an Official Handbook *in the 1920s detailing their services in the Buxton, Macclesfield, and Stockport areas, with descriptions and Illustrations of each route. The cover featured a Y-type Daimler in a rural setting.*

Above right
The cover of the 1959 North Western timetable had much in keeping with the Handbook, *but now with a Leyland Royal Tiger bus on the cover and no illustrations.*

today. However, the need then was not for the current environmental reasons but to produce a smoother form of transmission, the traditional clutch and gearbox being eliminated and replaced by a petrol engine, powering a dynamo driving an electric motor which would provide a smooth drive to the rear axle. So between 1924 and 1931 it was virtually inevitable that nearly all vehicles bought new by North Western would be Tillings. They became known as 'Tinkling Tillings', the sound thought to be caused by the starting handle vibrating. The refining of gear box and clutch systems resulted in the later Tilling-Stevens productions having conventional gearboxes.

THE BRISTOL ERA

The first Bristols arrived in 1936, with the Bristol chassis building works now part of the Tilling group, and North Western virtually standardising on Gardner 5LW-engined Bristol chassis up to 1950 for both single and double-deckers, mostly with Eastern Coach Works (ECW) bodies. This chassis/body/engine combination was to become a classic combination nationwide. The end of hostilities determined that from 1946 onwards for some seven years, North Western would embark on an extensive overhauling and re-bodying of pre-war Bristol chassis, the company obviously being impressed with the rugged reliability of the chassis, particularly when powered by the equally reliable Gardner 5LW engine.

PURCHASING CHANGES

The situation concerning the purchase of new vehicles would change drastically however following the Transport Act of 1947. The decision to rationalise Tilling and BAT shared ownership of many operators by exchanging shares resulted in operators becoming part of one or the other holding company, North

Above
Following their absorption into BET Group, the last year North Western was able to purchase Bristol L5Gs was in 1950. CDB 206 is from the batch delivered the previous year with a Weymann body. Alongside it (and both in the Quantock Heritage Fleet) is AJA 132. With a chassis dating from 1938, AJA 132 was rebodied in 1950/1 by Burlingham, as part of the rebodying programme North Western undertook.

Western becoming part of the BET group. The establishment of the British Transport Commission (BTC) would result in all the Tilling companies being sold out to the government, including Bristol and ECW, and their products would no longer be available to any organisations outside the nationalised group. The next few years would see North Western purchasing a variety of vehicles, including chassis made by Atkinson, AEC, Leyland, Dennis and Albion. Eventually former North Western Bristol, Leyland, and AEC examples would be represented in the Quantock fleet.

Above
AEC Reliance RDB 846 in the Quantock fleet, one of twenty delivered to North Western in 1963 with Alexander bodies, the first of many Alexander bodied vehicles the Company would operate.

Above left
CDB 206 while with North Western, withdrawn by them in 1963.

Left
While in service with North Western and with its original ECW body having been replaced by Burlingham, AJA 132 would have given a total of some twenty-three years in service before withdrawal by North Western in 1961.

A TIGER CUB AND A RELIANCE

The 1950s onwards saw North Western purchasing primarily Leyland and AEC chassis, including a second batch of Leyland Tiger Cubs in 1960 with dual-purpose Willowbrook bodies, thus making them suitable for long distance services. Following withdrawal by North Western, LDB 796, a 1960 Leyland Tiger Cub, eventually spent some time with a Dutch owner before re-joining the Quantock Fleet (see page 78).

In 1961, North Western purchased a batch of twenty AEC Reliances with Alexander bodies, RDB 832-861. Essentially a bus body shell, they were classed as coaches and originally were painted in North Western's all-over cream coach livery with a red waist band. Fitted with high-backed coach seats, high-geared rear axles, and cove windows, they were suitable for express services as well as private hire work. They were also fitted with folding air-operated front doors, allowing them to be converted to bus duties in 1968. Becoming part of the SELNEC fleet after withdrawal, RDB 846 eventually joined the Quantock Heritage fleet, before being sold on for further preservation.

FRANK COWLEY AND NORTH WESTERN

The role that Frank Cowley, the Salford based second-hand vehicle dealer, played in the history of North Western has rarely been mentioned, yet from 1946 up to North Western being absorbed into the SELNEC fleet, Cowley took nearly all of North Western's redundant vehicles, including the two Bristol L5Gs which eventually joined Quantock Heritage. Cowley forwarded many vehicles on to smaller operators and contractors, possibly on some form of 'lease-hire' system, as vehicles did appear to return to him for final disposal.

Other dealers Cowley disposed of vehicles to included Jack Broadhead of Bollington, some few miles south of North Western's main premises in Stockport. Broadhead was an operator/dealer who was taken over by North Western in 1938 but who continued operating as a dealer.

Above
Frank Cowley had premises on Blackfriars Bridge, linking Salford with Manchester. Vehicles such as North Western CDB 205 could be seen there for sale, hopefully attracting customers passing on this main north-south route in pre-Motorway days. CDB 205, originally fleet number 205, but with fleet number and North Western name removed, looks to be in very sound condition and, with a Gardner engine, good for many more miles.

Right
The cost of the 117 vehicles offered for sale by Frank Cowley in this advertisement range from £225 to £395 each, the latter being for Bristol vehicles.

Inset
A poor quality box camera snap looks into Cowley's south Manchester yard in Fallowfield. An ex-army armoured car guards the entrance. Behind is a line-up of ex.-North Western L5G's, with a mixture of Windover coach and ECW bus bodies, all withdrawn by 1960.

FRANK COWLEY
3, BLACKFRIARS ROAD,
SALFORD 3, ENGLAND
TELEPHONE: MANCHESTER BLACKFRIARS 7577

ALL THE FOLLOWING VEHICLES ARE OFFERED FOR EXPORT AND EVERY FACILITY WILL BE GIVEN FOR OVERSEAS BUYERS TO INSPECT AND ROAD TEST SAME. DELIVERY TO DOCKS FREE OF CHARGE

31 1938/39 T.S.8 **LEYLAND** Diesel-engined 34-seater buses, in good mechanical condition, with very good bodies and seats.

20 **BEDFORD** 1942/43/44 Utility 28/30-seater buses in A1 condition throughout, ready for work. £320 each.

45 **LEYLAND** 30/31-seater luxury coaches, fitted with Leyland petrol engines. These are a very fine fleet of vehicles and include a full store of spare parts for same. £325 each.

10 **LEYLAND** 34-seater service buses, in excellent mechanical condition, 1946-built bodies mounted on the famous T.S.4 petrol-engined chassis, all complete with good batteries and good tyres, ideal for conveyance of workmen, etc., ready to put into service. £225 each.

3 **DENNIS** 31-seater coaches with very sound Eastern Counties bodies, powered by Dennis famous Big 4 Diesel engine and fitted with a 5-speed gear box, full complement of spare parts for same. £350 each.

8 **BRISTOL** chassis, "L" type, powered by Gardner 4-cylinder Diesel oil engines and fitted with exceptionally good 32-seater bus bodies. £395 each.

We have over 200 passenger-carrying [...] Bedford, Dodge, Bristol [...] ments or send for co[...] lowest in England.

All makes of second-han[...] timber logging, etc.

FRAN[...]
3, BLA[...]
SALFO[...], ENGLAND
TELEPHONE: MANCHESTER BLACKFRIARS 7577

In 1951, Stockport Corporation Transport took delivery of twenty-four Leyland Titan PD2/1s with Leyland H30/26R bodies. They were chiefly purchased along with a batch of Crossley bodied Crossleys to meet the final closure of the tramway system on routes such as 17 Stockport to Reddish. It is likely that the Crossleys were purchased because of a local authority decision to support local industry and had the Transport Department been able to have their own way, the 1951 purchase would likely have been all-Leyland. Most of the batch became part of the SELNEC (Southern) fleet in 1969, with some dispersed to other SELNEC divisions. However, EDB 549 (295) enjoyed a different history.

Over the years, the need to lop trees in the Borough had resulted in various vehicles being used for such purposes, including JA 7626 (226), a 1949 Crossley DD42/3, which, following a crash, had its top removed. Eventually, 226 was replaced by EDB 549 (295), which was similarly converted and used. Initially, the roof and upper deck windows were removed and a handrail fitted. On being transferred to SELNEC in 1969, the bus was repainted in SELNEC livery, fitted with a transparent screen to cover the upper deck front and front nearside and offside panels, and re-seated. As such, it was used by SELNEC for private hire work until finally passing to the Museum of Transport, Manchester. Serious deterioration in the rear open platform and staircase areas had developed over the years. Following purchase from the Museum by Quantock Heritage, staircase steel side panelling and framework as well as

Left
The Museum of Transport had commenced work to rebuild the rear platform when the bus became part of the Quantock Fleet. Replacement steel angle sections supporting the floor were fitted and the platform floor replaced. The staircase steel panelling and framework as well as the staircase itself were rebuilt. Electrics in the cab were found to be in a poor state and needed replacement, much of the wiring having fused together.

the staircase itself were rebuilt. At the same time, the electrics particularly in the cab were found to be in a poor state, much of the wiring having fused together. This resulted in 295 being rewired, including replacing the rotten wooden unit housing the rear stop and taillights. The remainder of the body overall was sound and mechanically the bus was in good condition. One aspect of the engine was perhaps unusual in that an Autovac was fitted. Commonly found on pre-war vehicles, later designs of fuel pump rendered Autovacs unnecessary. Autovacs were made in Stockport so perhaps their fitting was more about supporting local industry than mechanical necessity. Along with EDB 549, two other former Quantock vehicles are now under new ownership in Kaunas, Lithuania; Blue Bus Daimler COG5/40 GNU 750 and Southern Vectis Bristol Lodekka BAS 563.

Above left
Reseated and with a transparent screen fitted to the front of the upper deck, 295 is now with SELNEC (as can be seen with the sticker on the side) but is yet to be repainted into SELNEC livery.

Above right
295 converted to an open-topper by Stockport Corporation Transport, used as for lopping trees and as a driver training vehicle. (Photograph courtesy of John Fozzard)

Right
Restoration completed and in the Quantock Fleet.

Above
LDB 796 (fleet number 796) was one of a batch of fifteen Leyland Tiger Cubs delivered to North Western in 1960. They were fitted with Willowbrook dual purpose bodywork seating 45. They earned the name 'black tops'. North Western had experimented on a 1952 Leyland Royal Tiger Coach with a similar red and black livery. 796 became part of the SELNEC fleet, and when disposed of by them had a number of preservationist owners before joining Quantock Heritage. One was a school teacher who occasionally delighted his pupils by 'commuting' to school in it! It was re-upholstered with another owner by an upholsterer who had worked for North Western.

Above
It had been pre-war practice for coaches to be fitted with accommodation on the roof to carry luggage. As vehicle design changed and it was possible to provide increased space in vehicle side lockers, the need for roof luggage racks diminished. Royal Blue continued to specify roof racks on their vehicles (including OTT 96) into the post-war period. However, the roof racks did not detract from the elegant lines of the ECW body.

After a spell abroad with a Dutch preservationist/operator it was agreed to bring back into the Heritage fleet the ex-North Western Leyland Tiger Cub LDB 796 by exchanging it for an ex-Royal Blue Bristol LS6G, OTT 96. The foundation of the Royal Blue Express Coach Services Company can be traced back to 1880, when Thomas Elliott first obtained a hackney carriage licence in Bournemouth.

Joined later by his sons, the company established a high reputation under the Royal Blue name, becoming the major tour operator in Bournemouth and particularly establishing express service to London. Agreement was reached with Hants and Dorset that Royal Blue would not compete with them on stage carriage services and expansion of express services continued. Financial and other considerations

determined that Royal Blue would be sold to the Tilling Group in 1935. The express services would be operated by Southern and Western National, also part of the Tilling Group, with those of Royal Blue in a revised Royal Blue livery of dark blue and cream. Under the formation of the National Bus Company in 1969, Royal Blue would become part of the National Express network.

AEC Reliance MU3RV
200 APB (1956)
Burlingham B44F
(Safeguard, Guildford)

Daimler CVG6LX-30
572 CNW (1962)
Roe H39/31F
(Leeds Corporation) but painted in Huddersfield colours

Daimler COG5/40
GNU 750 (1939)
Willowbrook C35F
(Blue Bus Services)

Daimler CVD6/SD
CHL 772 (1950)
Willowbrook B35F
(Bullocks, B & S, Featherstone)

Dennis Lancet J3
CFN 121 (1949)
Park Royal B35R
(East Kent)

AEC Reliance 2MU3RV
890 ADV (1959)
Willowbrook C31F
(Devon General/Grey Cars)

Since Steve Morris first became involved with bus and coach preservation a large variety of vehicle types representing Private, Company, and Corporation ownership have been found in the Quantock Heritage fleet and its predecessor, Rexquote Heritage Motor Services. The photographs here give some indication of this variety. Though they have not been covered in this book, all have a story to tell.

AEC Regal 111
ACH 441 (1948)
Windover C32F
(originally Trent then Burtons)

Bristol FLF6G
DEL 893C (1965)
E.C.W. H38/32F
(Hants & Dorset)

Bought for Spares!

Leyland Tiger PS1/1
KUP 949 (1950)
Burlingham C33F
(Iveson, Co. Durham)

AEC Regal 111
JUP 233 (1948)
Burlingham B35F
(Gillett Bros., Co. Durham)

AEC Reliance 2MU3RV
805 EVT (1960)
Weymann DP41F
(PMT)

  TECHNICAL VARIETY DENNIS BROS LTD GUILDFORD ENGLAND

Crossley DD42/7 Crossley HOE 8 litre engine

4 speed constant mesh gearbox

Vacuum brakes

(see the Demise of Crossley Motors. Crossley EVD 406)

Dennis Lancet J3 Dennis O6 7.5 litre engine

4-speed constant mesh gearbox

Vacuum brakes

(see previous page CFN 121)

Daimler CVD6 Daimler CD6 8.4 litre engine

4-speed pre-selector gearbox

Vacuum brakes

(see previous page CHL 772)

Leyland Tiger PS1/1 Leyland E181 7.4 litre engine

4-speed constant mesh gearbox

Vacuum brakes

(see previous page KUP 949 and The Early Days Crosville)

Leyland Tiger Cub PSUC1/1 Leyland 5.7 litre engine

4-speed constant mesh gearbox

Air brakes

(see The Demise of Crossley Motors. Leyland Tiger Cub NDB 356)

AEC Regal 111 AEC 173 7.7 litre engine

4- speed constant mesh gearbox.

Vacuum brakes

(see previous page ACH 441, JUP 233)

AEC Reliance AEC AH470 7.6 litre engine

Synchromesh gearbox

Air brakes

(see previous page 200 APB, 890 ADV, 805 EVT)

Many of the vehicles in the Quantock fleet past and present have both chassis and engines made by Leyland or AEC. Within those and other manufacturers' products some of the variations to be found are indicated in the text. Others are detailed above along with engines featured in the Vehicle Variety pages. It can be seen that Quantock Heritage have had to cope with a wide variety of engines and gearboxes from different manufactures. Gearboxes could include synchromesh, constant mesh ('crash'), and pre-select, necessitating any drivers working for Quantock needing a wide variety of driving skills and experience! Quick gear changes were possible in a constant mesh box if a clutch stop was fitted. This could be invaluable particularly when moving away on a hill start. Many engine components could be found in common across a range of vehicles. Equipment such as starter motors, fuel pumps, dynamos, clutch plates, electrical and other equipment including major fittings such as axles would mostly be supplied by specialist companies such as CAV, Simms, Borg and Beck, and Kirkstall. Leyland and AEC in particular invariably promoted their own engines when operators were purchasing new vehicles. The many different design specifications would lead to a complexity of parts and detailed descriptions in both their and other manufacturers' service and spares manuals. Other chassis manufacturers would offer their own engines or one from another engine builder, in particular those made by the diesel engine manufacturer L. Gardner of Patricroft in Manchester.

The origin of L.Gardner & Sons can be traced back to the late 1860s, becoming in due course best known for their LW series of diesel engines. Although making their own engines, Bristol, Dennis, Daimler and other manufacturers would supply their chassis fitted particularly in the early pre- and post-war periods with the Gardner 5LW or 6LW version. The 5LW became the most well-known of the LW series, with Bristol most commonly fitting it to their L (single deck) and K (double deck) half cab chassis. Over the years, the Quantock fleet has included a number of Bristol Ls, from the North Western and Crosville fleets. One ex-Crosville Bristol L however (featured on the cover, GFM 882) is an L6A, i.e. fitted with an AEC 7.7 litre engine (see Technical Variety). Sadly, the manufacture of Gardner engines ceased in 1997. The Company failed initially to introduce turbocharged engines in line with their competitors. They suffered from a lack of development funding and their larger engines were therefore less fuel efficient than their rivals and failed to meet EU emission standards.

Left
An early 5LW engine. The North Western and Crosville Bristol L5G's in the Quantock fleet used versions of this engine.
(Anson Museum Poynton)

Above
This Gardner advertisement from the late '50s features the 6LX (as fitted to 572 CNW shown in Vehicle Variety). Also featured is the horizontal version of the 5LW – the 5HLW- and the 4LK engine.

CCX 777

HUDDERSFIELD JOINT OMNIBUS COMMITTEE FLEET NUMBER 217

Daimler CWA6 with Duple lowbridge utility bodywork seating 55 people.

The C in the chassis designation purely stands for 'Commercial', the W indicating it was the war time chassis and the A6 denoting an AEC 6 cylinder engine. The Daimler chassis was in effect a wartime version of the pre-war chassis which had been in quantity production from 1934 to 1940. This basically reflected the replacement of certain aluminium alloy components by cast iron; the back axle was a 'bought in' unit rather than a Daimler produced one. The fluid flywheel and preselect gearbox of the pre-war model were retained; this particular arrangement allowed the driver to select a gear before making the change, the actual change was only made when he depressed the gear change pedal which took the place of the clutch pedal for a normal manual gearbox.

Before tracing the history of this particular bus, a little bit of background information is first required.

Above
Not CCX 777 but identical CCX 778 in what looks like an official publicity shot when new. (Huddersfield Passenger Transport Collection)

HUDDERSFIELD JOINT OMNIBUS COMMITTEE

To trace the origins of the Joint Omnibus Committee it is necessary to go right back to 1880 when an Act of Parliament gave the County Borough of Huddersfield powers to construct tramways. At this time, it had been intended that municipalities would lay the necessary track, but actual trams and services would be provided by a private company. Probably because of the difficult operating terrain, no operator could be found, so a licence to operate trams was obtained by the Borough itself and Huddersfield became the first municipality to construct and operate its own tramway system. Initially using steam trams supplemented with horse trams, work was started in 1899 to convert the whole system to electric traction and completed in 1902. Over the ensuing years, the system developed, with the appropriate permissions, to include routes into the areas of the surrounding authorities. In 1913, powers were obtained to run motor buses within the Borough but the First World War intervened and no developments took place. However, the Huddersfield Corporation (General Powers) Act of 1920 not only granted permission to construct additional tramways but also authorised the use of motor buses on certain routes outside the Borough. During the 1920s, bus services were expanded throughout the area including links to neighbouring Bradford and Halifax.

The growth of bus services throughout the country had not gone unnoticed by the railway companies, with traffic loss particularly seen on short distance urban routes. However, the railways knew that their powers to run bus services were doubtful and thus promoted a Bill in Parliament to allow them to operate road passenger vehicles. Once granted under the Railways (Road Transport) Act of 1928, the action they took was to buy into the already

Left
The vehicles carried a combination of the Huddersfield crest, based on the Ramsden family crest who had held the manor of Huddersfield since the time of Elizabeth I and played a major part in the development of the town, and that of the LMS railway featuring a winged cross of St George, presumably to represent travel, an English rose and a Scottish thistle. What the Yorkshire folk thought of a red, rather than white rose, is not known.

established major company operators rather than start their own services. As seen above, Huddersfield Corporation had developed bus services beyond their municipal boundaries and thus was approached by the London, Midland & Scottish Railway (LMS) for a slice of the action.

On 16 May 1930, an agreement was entered into between Huddersfield Corporation and the LMS; the railway purchased a half share in the motor bus section of the Corporation Tramways Department and together they formed the Huddersfield Joint Omnibus Committee to run the motor bus services. It should be noted that the electric tramways remained solely owned by Huddersfield Corporation. The buses became equally owned by the Corporation and the Railway, but it is understood that the arrangement was that all buses with an even

number in their registration were Corporation owned, whereas those with an odd number were owned by the Railway; the actual owner was reflected in the legal lettering on the individual vehicles. With railway nationalisation in 1948, the LMS share was to pass to British Railways.

Throughout the 1930s, the Huddersfield Corporation trams were replaced by trolleybuses, with the final tram running in June 1940. In turn, the trolleybuses came to be replaced by buses, with the changeover completed in July 1968. These replacement buses were to be solely owned by the Corporation and not part of the Joint Omnibus fleet.

Railway Joint Omnibus Committees were only a Yorkshire 'thing', with similar but certainly not identical set ups in Todmorden, Halifax and Sheffield.

To complete the story, the 1968 Transport Act meant that the railways' shareholding in the Joint Omnibus Committee was transferred to the then newly created National Bus Company. This however was short lived as on 1 April 1969, Huddersfield Corporation purchased the National Bus Company interest. Huddersfield Corporation itself became part of the West Yorkshire Passenger Transport Executive in 1974. To comply with the 1985 Transport Act, an 'arm's length' company, Yorkshire Rider, was formed in 1986. It was subject to a management buy-out in 1989 but was purchased by Badgerline in 1994 and thus became part of First Group who, today, continues to provide many of the services in the area.

UTILITY BUSES

During the early part of the Second World War, bus production had ground to a halt as manufacture for the military was obviously taking top priority. It was however recognised that new buses would be needed if essential services, such as transport of war workers, were to be maintained.

All manufacture in the country was under the control of the Ministry of Supply (MoS) to ensure that the war effort was as effective as possible. Initially, the MoS gave permission for completion of vehicles for which stocks of parts were available. Under this initiative, around 350 double-deckers and 60 single-deckers were produced and these were to become known as the 'unfrozen' buses. The allocation of buses to operators was on the basis of need and controlled by the Ministry of War Transport (MoWT), and this would continue for the duration of the war.

As a more long term measure to ensure a supply of new buses, a group was set up by the MoS and MoWT in 1941, with the rather long title of the National Federation of Vehicle Trades & Operators Joint Technical Advisory Group, with the remit to produce plans for new buses which used a minimum amount of materials and skilled labour. The result was a set of designs for very basic vehicles (double-deckers (high and lowbridge), single-decker and trolleybus) devoid of any unnecessary fittings and styling features. Aluminium was required for aircraft production so was replaced wherever possible with steel, double curvature of roof domes was eliminated to save skilled panel beating. No window pans were included, with glazing directly within the body framing. Interior side and roof lining panels were omitted and the number of opening windows was severely reduced. Wooden slatted, rather than upholstered, seating was also to figure from 1943. These specifications were the 'Utility' bus.

In practice, the bodybuilders allocated the work produced their own distinctive styles within the constraints imposed. By 1944, the situation regarding material and labour had eased and changes to the specifications were introduced and the overall term 'Relaxed Utilities' came to be used for these later vehicles. A certain amount of aluminium was now available to replace steel panelling, curved front and rear roof domes were again allowed, additional opening windows and the reintroduction of upholstered seats. The actual availability of materials remained erratic and there was a wide variation both in time and extent by which the changes could be introduced by individual manufacturers.

For double-deckers, the chassis were originally to be all supplied by Guy Motors of Wolverhampton but later on Daimler and to a lesser extent Bristol were allowed to resume chassis manufacture.

The Daimler factory in Coventry had been badly damaged in air raids and production was only possible again when the MoS requisitioned

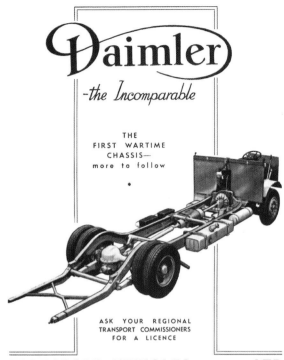

Above
Advertisement for the Daimler chassis from the contemporary trade press. It is not quite known why the chassis was advertised, because at the time one would not really have had a choice but got what you were given.

a factory in Wolverhampton. Therefore, despite general efforts to disperse wartime manufacture, all double-deck chassis production ended up in one town! Only Gardner engines were initially available but later on, supplies of AEC engines were also released.

With the end of the war in 1945, the control of production and allocation of new buses to operators was gradually eased, although this was still in a climate of material shortages.

Above
No.217 in service in Huddersfield, but confusingly carrying the number plate, and likely the whole radiator from CCX 661, No. 205 one of the Brush bodied examples. This was no doubt a temporary fix to cover accident damage or repair and the number plates were not swapped over. I wonder what it said on the back of the bus? (R. Mack, courtesy Geoff Lumb)

Above
Talking of accident damage, here is No. 217 after an argument with a cattle truck sometime around 1950. The repair will have tested the skills of the Huddersfield workshops. (Geoff Lumb)

The Huddersfield Joint Omnibus Committee was allocated twenty utility buses during the war by the MoWT; these were all Daimler CWA6 chassis, thirteen with bodies by Duple, of Hendon and seven by Brush of Loughborough. All were of lowbridge configuration except for one Duple highbridge example. The lowbridge buses allowed extra capacity on routes that were otherwise restricted to single-deckers.

These buses were delivered in ones and twos in the period between October 1943 and August 1945, with No. 217, CCX 777, arriving in July 1945. Therefore, the Duple body was able to incorporate the relaxed utility specifications; the rear dome was more rounded, additional opening windows were incorporated, with the added luxury of upholstered seats and a little bit of interior varnished wood trim. Having an odd

numbered registration, No. 217 was therefore owned by the LMS.

Most of the wartime Daimlers were to remain in service with the Joint Omnibus Committee until the mid-1950s, with many of them then passing to other owners throughout the country for further service. No. 217 was no exception and, with No. 219, CCX 779, was sold in 1955 for further municipal service in West Bridgford, Nottinghamshire.

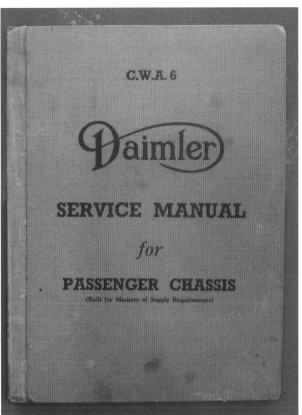

Above left
The AEC advertisement is from just after the war, when supplies were short, but there was beginning to be a return to a bit of choice.

Above right
The service manual, a must for all vehicle owners and operators.

West Bridgford lies immediately to the south of the city of Nottingham, separated only by the River Trent, and now effectively making it a suburb of the city; however, from the nineteenth century it had become established as a separate urban district. In 1913, Nottingham obtained powers to expand their tramways and also operate buses and trolleybuses, and to counteract this, the Urban District Council obtained powers to operate their own motor buses; and thus the West Bridgford Urban District Council Passenger Transport Department came into being. The West Bridgford buses initially terminated at the Trent Bridge tram terminus, on the north side of the River Trent until 1927, when an agreement was reached with Nottingham City Council and a joint transport area between the two local authorities was established.

At the end of the war, like many large cities, there was an extreme shortage of housing in Nottingham as a result of bomb damage and the need for slum clearance. In October 1945, the City Council approved the acquisition of nearly 1,000 acres of land for housing in Clifton to the south of the river and west of West Bridgford. Planning permission was granted in 1951 and homes for 30,000 people

were constructed between that year and 1960, making this development at the time Europe's largest council housing estate. Obviously there was demand from the new residents for bus services and in the early days this was provided by the independent operator South Notts. Bus Co. Ltd. existing route from Nottingham to Loughborough and Gotham. However, Nottingham Corporation Transport had eyes on this lucrative traffic in to and out of the city and applied to the Traffic Commissioners for a route to the estate. Nottingham was awarded 47 per cent, West Bridgford 28 per cent and South Notts. 25 per cent of the service to the estate, which started as a single route, numbered 61;

later this developed into five routes with differing terminal points in the estate.

Initially, the route had to cross the river at Trent Bridge (the only major crossing for at least ten miles in either direction) and therefore into West Bridgford before proceeding to Clifton. On this latter stretch, the route encountered a low and narrow railway bridge which required the use of lowbridge double-deckers. The service commenced in October 1952, with Nottingham

Right
Loaded up, driver with hand on the brake lever, and ready to set off for Clifton. Note the addition of the side route number box and modifications to the upper deck front windows have not yet been made. (Ray Pettit collection)

Corporation using seven lowbridge Duple bodied Daimler CWA6 vehicles bought from Bradford Corporation. West Bridgford initially had three pre-war Park Royal AEC Regents (hurriedly converted to lowbridge layout by Willowbrook) and these were supplemented in 1955 by the two Daimlers purchased from Huddersfield at a cost of £800. CCX 777 and 779 were numbered 24 and 27 respectively and it is interesting to note that they were to a similar specification to the ex-Bradford vehicles used by Nottingham. No. 27 entered service in May 1955 (still in Huddersfield livery) and No. 24 one month later.

When the new Clifton Bridge over the River Trent was opened in 1958, Nottingham Corporation buses shortened their route to Clifton by using the new bridge, avoiding Trent Bridge and the low railway bridge. A fleet of forty-four new Leyland PD2s with Metro-Cammell highbridge bodies had been acquired specially for the new services. Thus, South Notts and WBUDC had the services via Trent Bridge to themselves, though Barton also had an hourly working on route 54 which operated to Clifton via Ruddington.

The two Daimlers went on to give thirteen years' service with West Bridgford; and *Buses Illustrated* magazine of December 1967 recorded the final withdrawal of No. 24, CCX 777. Also noted in the magazine was the arrival of AEC Swift single-deckers in the fleet; so very different replacements from a very different era. CCX 777 must have been the last utility in virtually original condition still in revenue earning service. Its existence had not gone unnoticed by

the enthusiast fraternity and it was purchased for preservation. In fact, an advertisement in the March 1967 copy of *Buses Illustrated* recalls fundraising in advance of withdrawal. The lucky new owner was given the bus as a 21st birthday present! CCX 779 was not so fortunate and went to a local dealer, presumably for scrap, in July 1967.

MARCH 1967

SMALL ADVERTISEMENTS

Announcements in this column cost 3d per word S.A.E. if acknowledgement required. Copy and remittance to: Buses Illustrated, Classified Advertisement Dept., Terminal House, Shepperton, Middx., to arrive not later than 25th of any month. The publishers retain the right to refuse or withdraw advertisements at their discretion and they do not accept liability for omissions, clerical or printers errors, or for the bona fides of advertisers, although every care is taken to avoid mistakes, and advertisements from doubtful sources.

OPERATIONS CLERK required, good wages and excellent prospects in expanding organisation. Some shift work involved. L.V's, pension scheme, concessional holidays abroad. Apply Traffic Manager, Charles Rickards (Tours) Ltd., Glenhurst Road, Brentford, Mdx. Isl. 4511, ext. 2.

"PENNYFARE" and "London Transport Magazine" from October 1939 for sale. Also London bus and coach maps (including Coronation 1937 and 1953), some pre-war and country bus and coach post-war timetables. S.A.E. for list to A. P. Brentnall, 63 Victoria Road, Addlestone, Surrey.

50 DIFFERENT TICKETS 1s 6d. A. Pearce, 75 Thornton Crescent, Wendover, Bucks.

URGENTLY REQUIRED. Pre 1955 Dinky Double-Deck buses. Details and suggested price to J. C. Tebb, 133 High Street, Yeadon, Leeds.

VISIT TO BARTON'S, Skill's, West Bridgford U.D.C. and Gash's. Sunday 19th March. Depart Nottingham 11.30 a.m. Profits towards preservation of West Bridgford 24, to be used for tour. Details s.a.e. to J. R. Denham, Cripps Hall, University Park, Nottingham.

In the following years, CCX 777 was very active on the then growing bus rally circuit of the 1970s.

Work carried out during this period included reverting to the original fixed upper deck front windows, return to Huddersfield JOC colours and a restoration of the interior. There were also appearances in the long running *Last of the Summer Wine* comedy series on the BBC. However, over the years, for a variety of circumstances, appearances of CCX 777 became less frequent and eventually it went into hibernation.

Emerging from storage and arriving with Quantock in Somerset in 2006, CCX 777 presented a basically complete bus though looking rather dusty and neglected. Work on the AEC engine was required to make it mechanically sound again. The interior presented a certain patina of a bus that had worked hard for its living and this is retained. The only major work that has been necessary here has been the replacement of cracked and broken linoleum flooring in the upper deck offside sunken gangway and sections of some of the underlying floorboards. The exterior paintwork was however too poor to be rescued and the rectification of this found to be necessary.

Above
Early days down in Somerset after a good clean.

Freshly painted in all over red of PMT and with advertisements of the time and place completing the picture.

CCX 777 reappeared as Potteries Motor Traction (PMT) fleet number B58 (registration KEH 8), to rekindle youthful memories from Steve Morris's home town of Stoke on Trent. KEH 8 was one of ten Duple lowbridge bodied Daimler CWA6 built in 1945-46 and supplied to the independent operator Brown's Motor Company (Tunstall) Ltd. After the war, PMT pursued a vigorous policy of acquiring many of the numerous independent operators in the area and Brown's were taken over in 1952. Eight of the ten Daimlers were rebodied in 1954 with Northern Counties lowbridge bodies but two, one being KEH 8, kept their original relaxed utility bodies. The B prefix to the fleet number indicated it was originally a Brown's vehicle and this was retained until a wholesale fleet numbering in the mid-1950s, when the number L285 was allocated; the prefix in this instance now indicating a lowbridge vehicle.

Joules Stone Ales; Stone refers to the location of the brewery in the town of Stone just to the south of Stoke on Trent. Like many local concerns the business was acquired by Bass/Charrington in the 1970s and the brewery demolished. However, the name has recently been independently resurrected and brewing recommenced, though this time just over the border into Shropshire at Market Drayton.

Huntbach's was a large department store whose origins can be traced back to a small shop opened in Hanley by Michael Huntbach in 1861. By the early 1970s, the store had been replaced by a branch of the national chain, Littlewood's. Michael Huntbach also played a big part in civic life, he became a local councillor in 1871 and was elected mayor for several periods in the 1890's and 1900's; he even had a street named after him.

Tizer was of course well known as one of the staple drinks of the young bus spotter. Its origins go back to Pickup's Appetizer launched in Manchester in 1924; still available today and produced by the Barr's group whose other products include Irn Bru.

All pictures (Bob Brimley)

AT WORK IN THE POTTERIES

Left
The real KEH 8 with Brown's of Tunstall, not a very clear shot but seems to suit the times. The colour scheme was appropriately brown and white. (Roy Marshall collection)

Right
KEH 7 this time and a much clearer picture. Note the roundabout sign and the rather fine gas lamp. (Roy Marshall)

Above
The real KEH 8 again and now part of the PMT fleet in the overall red colour scheme and the inspiration for the CCX 777 repaint. The driver leans across to consult with the conductor sporting a TIM (Ticket Issuing Machine). Meanwhile, upstairs at the front, a passenger demonstrates the awkward manoeuvre from the long bench seat into the sunken gangway. The number plate has been moved to below the cab window and there is now a shiny polished radiator surround. (Roy Marshall)

Above right
A later shot of KEH 8, featuring a livery which had introduced cream window surrounds and roof. The front upper deck has been rebuilt and the windows are now mounted in rubber gaskets. This could be the result of accident damage or an attempt to eke a bit more life out of the body; utility bodies often did not prove very durable because properly seasoned timber had not always been available. Passengers queue patiently as an elderly lady struggles with the step up onto the platform.

After a couple of seasons, CCX 777 was to be transformed again, this time into a London Transport bus. The reason for this was a request to participate in a Running Day in August 2008 based on Worcester Park in south-west London. The date marked the 50th anniversary of the withdrawal of London's first red bus (Central Area) route operated by lowbridge double-deckers. The bridge requiring such vehicles was at Worcester Park railway station, the route was the 127, and its demise was a result of cuts following the long bus strike of 1958. Previously a single deck route numbered 245, wartime demands for transport to/from local factories required greater capacity and in 1941 the 245 became the 127. At this time, most of London's lowbridge double-deckers were required on country area routes and those few that could be spared were initially supplemented by others borrowed from Manchester Corporation. Eventually, in 1944, London Transport was able to obtain some Daimler CWA6s with Duple lowbridge bodies, these being numbered D1-6, followed by a second batch, D128-131, received in November 1945. In total London received 281 Daimler wartime double-deckers, all the others being highbridge type. D1-6 and 128-131 were to spend their entire time in London almost exclusively on route 127 until withdrawn and replaced in 1952 by members of the AEC Regent III/Weymann lowbridge RLH class vehicles.

As none of London's wartime Daimlers had survived, CCX 777 was called on to represent their era on route 127 at the event. CCX 777 is closer in age to the second batch and the fleet number D130 (original registration HGC 257) was selected. This was mainly because D130 was the only one of the four that was repainted into the all-over red livery relieved with just a between decks cream band. The other three all retained the earlier livery of red with white window surrounds and brown roof. 'Conversion' of CCX 777 was therefore more straightforward from the all over PMT red livery. Appropriate fleet names and numbers were applied and the local adverts for the Stoke on Trent area replaced. Following withdrawal from service in London, many of the wartime Daimlers,

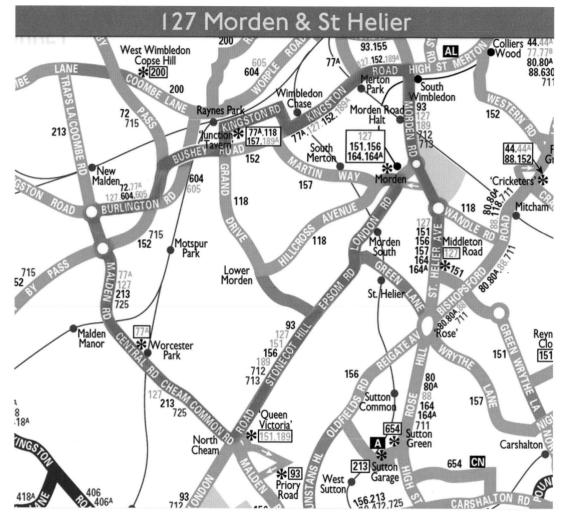

(Mike Harris, busmap.co.uk)

including D130, were exported to what was then Ceylon, now Sri Lanka, where they no doubt endured a very hard time. During this later life there would be rebuilding or rebodying, with some eventually converted to lorries and lasted in this form into the 1980s.

The 127 was a strange shaped route and is best illustrated by the map above. Commencing from Morden, it almost completed a full circle to originally terminate at South Wimbledon; very close to its home garage of Merton (London Transport code AL). The extension to St Helier, a large London County Council housing estate, came later.

Above
CCX cheekily carrying the registration of D130, HGC 257, about to turn in to Worcester Park Station. The bridge in the background was the original requirement for lowbridge vehicles, though the road has since been lowered to make this unnecessary. (Keith Severn)

Above
The real D130 photographed in 1948, in North Cheam, and still in its original colour scheme. This is probably a warm day with the upper deck windows open and the driver has taken his hat off and hung it on the cab door pillar; one has to ask why there is an armchair on the pavement on the left-hand side of the photograph! (Alan B. Cross)

Above
Heeling over at a roundabout in New Malden, the semaphore indicator can be seen returning to its closed position. A Jacob's Cream Cracker advertisement has now been applied. The Cream Cracker was an Irish invention, first baked by William Jacob in around 1885. (Keith Severn)

Above
The real D130 again this time in the later all red livery. Standing outside Morden underground station with a full load on board and just waiting for the crew before setting off. (Alan B. Cross)

Above
Newly returned to Huddersfield JOC colours at the 2016 Taunton Vintage Bus day. (Dave Allen)

Above right and below
Looking towards the front on both decks at the relaxed utility interior. Very basic but the luxury again of upholstered seats and a little bit of varnished wood trim. (Dave Allen)

CCX 777 is once again back in Huddersfield JOC livery as befits its fifty years in preservation, but who knows what next? West Bridgford would be a prime candidate, but Southend also had lowbridge utility Daimlers in a nice pale blue and cream livery!

COASTAL COOPERATION

The East Kent Road Car Company, operating primarily in the south-east of the country, and Southdown Motor Services in the south-central area had begun, along with other operators particularly in the late 1930s, to build up a network of services stretching along the south coast. East Kent, by taking over other smaller operators, consolidated services from London to the Kent coast to such seaside resorts as Margate, Dover, and Ramsgate, as well as and in conjunction with Maidstone and District to inland destinations such as Canterbury and Maidstone. Also established in the 1930s in conjunction with the Royal Blue and Southdown companies, were express coastal services from Margate to Bournemouth, with a journey time of approximately twelve hours. Such services were through running, with crews from one company taking over a vehicle from another company at appropriate points, thus Royal Blue vehicles could be found as far east as Margate and East Kent as far west as Bournemouth.

Southdown, based in Brighton, had also established express services from the south/central part of the south coast from Brighton, Eastbourne and other centres to London as well as further into the Midlands. The development of all these and other express services would demand vehicles rather better then basic buses, and here the Leyland Tiger TS7 and TS8 chassis in particular came into their own. Leyland's Tiger

Above
Ex-East Kent Leyland Tiger JG 9938 in the Quantock Heritage fleet. The flat (silver painted) dumb irons either side of the bottom of the radiator distinguish the Tiger TS8 from the TS7. The radiator grille itself contained a series of vertical metal slats. These could be adjusted by a knob on the radiator to control the flow of air through the radiator.

JG 9938 was one of the three 1937/8 batch of Leyland TS8 coaches converted to use as mobile offices in 1957. JG 9937 and JG 9955 were disposed of in 1965 and 1967 respectively (parts of JG 9955 later being used in JG 9938's restoration). JG 9938 was allocated mobile office duties at Ferryfield Airport (Lydd), Folkstone Harbour and Reculver (where it is seen in the car park in May 1969). Its mobile office function ceased after 1970, the company restoring it externally in 1972 and using it for many official and promotional duties prior to is sale for preservation in 1979. (Richard Wallace)

Below
The Friends of King Alfred was one of very few groups brave enough to organise a winter running day based in Winchester on New Year's Day. Heritage vehicles were regular attendees at this event, and JG 9938 and East Kent Dennis Lancet CFN 121, also in the Quantock fleet, are seen about to depart for this event on what looks as if it might be a rather snowy journey!

TS7 chassis had grown in popularity during the 1930s, the TS8, with only minor differences to the TS7 being introduced in the summer of 1937. Both types were available with either petrol or diesel engines, although towards the end of the '30s, the TS8 with its 8.6 diesel engine was gaining popularity over petrol engines because of its greater fuel economy, and this was obviously a significant factor in running long distance express services. However, it was not unknown for large operators, having taken delivery of new diesel engined coaches, to remove the diesel engines on delivery and replace them with petrol engines from service buses, the buses receiving the new diesel engines. This was because the operators were aware that the petrol engines would be smoother and quieter running than their diesel counterparts, were faster (particularly on acceleration) and therefore more appropriate for coach work. Some operators, including Ribble Motor Services and Southdown continued to favour petrol engines.

Diesel engined Leyland Tiger TS8, JG 9938, was one of a batch of 35 delivered to East Kent in 1938/9 with Park Royal thirty-two seat, rear entrance coach bodies. With their high standard of internal finish, they were suitable for not only express services but also coaching duties. Between 1935 and 1937 Southdown received 90 Leyland Tiger TS7's fitted with coach bodies to a similar basic design built by Harrington, Beadle, Park Royal and Burlingham. Fleet number 1179, DUF 179, with Harrington body was one of the last to be supplied. Originally fitted with a petrol engine, it was replaced by a diesel unit in the early 1950's. Thomas Harrington was a long-established coach builder who over the years had built many bodies for Southdown – perhaps not surprising as both companies were based in Brighton. Harrington, along with J.S. Beadle was one of a small number of body builders

who, in the 1950's went on to produce integrally constructed vehicles. With their close links with the Rootes Group, Harrington worked with Commer to produce the Harrington Contender single deck integral vehicle in both bus and coach versions. This method of construction provided a body/chassis frame as a complete unit, to which all engine and running units were attached. The major advantage of such construction was lower overall weight, with reductions in fuel consumption. Harrington had also become famous for the 'dorsal fin' feature on many of its coach bodies, this being not only a styling feature but aiding saloon ventilation. Production of Harrington bodies finished in 1966 following a disastrous fire. On withdrawal, both 1179 and JG 9938 passed into preservation, in due course both joining the Heritage fleet.

RELIEVING A VEHICLE SHORTAGE

In 1948, although a BTC Company and duly bound to purchase the Bristol/ECW product, to help with a shortage of vehicles, Crosville took delivery of twelve AEC Regals with Strachans bodies. To ease the production pressure on ECW towards the end of the 1940s, Strachans had been commissioned by Tilling to build bodies to ECW specification. Basically similar to the ECW design, the Strachans body differed in various details, particularly in the window frames. Strachan & Brown, later becoming Strachans Successors, had started in London in 1921 as body builders and rapidly established a firm reputation for their products nationally with orders from municipal, company and private operators. In particular one customer – Aldershot & District – would remain loyal. Strachans' loss of them as customers, along with the nationalisation of the BET group, would severely affect their business, leading to their eventual closure in 1974. Towards the end, Strachans produced minibus bodies (eventually becoming known as 'bread vans') primarily on Ford Transit chassis, when operators were utilising such vehicles. Although producing a number of standard designs over the years, the Company was always happy to meet particular customers' requirements and specifications. Crosville were familiar with the AEC 7.7 engine as they already had Bristols so fitted, but the Regals, with their 4-speed boxes, proved to be less popular with the drivers than the Bristol single-deckers which

had 5-speed boxes. All the Strachan bodies on the Regals had to be extensively rebuilt after some years by Crosville. Whether or not this was the result of initial structural problems (including the possibility of unseasoned timber being used) is unknown, but it perhaps indicated the amount

of work which would have to be undertaken on JFM 575, the Regal which eventually joined the Quantock fleet. The above reasons were probably influential in the withdrawal of the whole batch by 1961, as well as them being by that time 'non-standard' in the Crosville fleet.

Above
JFM 575 seen shortly before removal from the farm in North Wales, and showing the deterioration which many years of standing in all weathers in open countryside had created. A bull was said to have smashed the headlights having seen its reflection in the glasses. It could be the one which looks on forlornly.

DANGER! BEWARE OF THE CATTLE!

Following withdrawal in 1961, JFM 575, fleet number TA5, was sold to a sea scout troop before being purchased by a farmer in Glan Conwy, North Wales. It was discovered there by a commercial airline pilot, David Moores, who flew regularly between the mainland and the Isle of Man and kept an eye on it for over twenty years. During that time, he also advised two enthusiast/preservationists of its existence, and, following a number of visits, they persuaded the farmer to let them notify the then DVLO, enabling the original registration number to be maintained. All too often when a vehicle is left derelict or remains off the road for years, unless appropriate action has been taken the original registration number is lost. Bought by the farmer originally for the engine for a project never carried out, it languished on the hills for a period of over forty years, not only at the mercy of the weather but a herd of cows rubbing up against one side of it. Had it not been rescued for preservation by Steve Morris for his Quantock Heritage fleet through the foresight of David Moores and other preservationists, it is likely JFM 575 would have eventually collapsed on its side, assisted not only by the weather but a herd of cattle!

Left
Partly winched and partly under its own steam following a 'snatch' from the farmer's tractor, the Regal is ready for its trip to Somerset. Much of the interior of the vehicle was missing, along with the rear end of the body as can be seen from the photo.

Right
With all flooring and panelling, both interior and exterior, having been removed, new framework has been constructed and fitted.

STEVE MORRIS WRITES:

'Following complete restoration, in 2006 TA5 was taken to the Crosville Centenary Rally in Llandudno, not far from the Welsh hillside where it had languished for so many years. The return visit of the Regal to North Wales was both highly emotional yet very satisfying. Two members of the family of Mr Roberts, the farmer who had owned the vehicle for so many years, came to see it. To say that they just couldn't believe it was the same old bus they had known semi-derelict on the farm for so long would be an understatement. They asked if they could arrange for other members of the family to see it, and later on, at the hotel in the Conwy Valley where we were staying prior to the return journey to Taunton, they turned up in force! They were amazed at the vehicle's transformation. It was a combination of delight and yet at the same time deep sorrow. There were lots of tears because, unfortunately, Mr Roberts had died before we had completed the restoration, and all the family were deeply upset that he was not there to see it. It was an experience which, I believe, totally vindicates what we do and makes it completely worthwhile.'

Above left
An early photograph of JFM 575 while with Crosville. This was before they had considerably rebuilt the pseudo-ECW Strachans bodies which had proved to be somewhat suspect in their structure, perhaps because unseasoned timber had been used in their construction.

Above right
Cab roof supported to prevent movement while cab being rebuilt.

Right
Since restoration, the AEC Regal has appeared frequently at rallies, particularly in the south west. It is seen here at Blue Anchor, on the West Somerset coast, not long after restoration.

PRODUCER GAS

In 1936, North Western commenced a long association with the Bristol/ECW combination. These were Bristol JO5Gs fitted with Eastern Coach Works 31 seat bus bodies with interiors finished to a high standard. One of the batch, JA 5528 (fleet number 728), eventually joined the Heritage collection after being dry stored for over fifty years as a potential restoration project. This bus had experienced an interesting history with North Western, having been converted to run on producer gas as a way of reducing liquid fuel consumption during the war years. The Ministry of Transport had issued a directive in 1942 requiring operators to so convert 10 per cent of their fleets. The method most commonly adapted (including by North Western) was to fit a trailer behind the vehicle carrying an anthracite burner producing a low-quality gas which could power adapted engines. The drawbacks of the system included problems of manoeuvrability as well as poor performance and limited mileage between refuelling. However North Western designed a unit to fit in the rear of a bus but 728, despite the advantages of not having to tow a trailer, was the only one so fitted. Excessive engine wear was experienced by engines adapted to run on producer gas. By 1944, the government scheme had been withdrawn, and all vehicles were eventually converted back to liquid fuel power.

Right
Following disposal by North Western to the dealer, Frank Cowley, 728 was subsequently used by a Welsh contractor before purchase for preservation by David Moores. David is an enthusiast and preservationist with a long-term interest particularly in the fleets of North Western and Crosville. Influential in the purchase for the Heritage fleet of ex-Crosville AEC JFM 575, David kept 728 in dry secure storage for over fifty years while undertaking other projects before donating it to the Quantock fleet. Some fifty years after being with the contractor, 728 still carries their fleet number.

REBODYING

Following the end of hostilities many operators including North Western found themselves with deteriorating fleets which had suffered through wartime pressures. As a result, many pre-war vehicles with chassis and engines which were sound or could be satisfactorily overhauled 'in house,' and were rebodied. Thus, North Western, apart from receiving new vehicles, would commence in 1946 a major rebodying programme which would continue in the 1950s.

Some of the first vehicles so treated were the 1936 ECW bodied Bristol JO5Gs, including 728, which received a new Brush body. The original ECW bodies were removed in the main garage in Charles St, Stockport and, following appropriate overhaul, the chassis were driven down to the Brush factory in Loughborough. Some of the ECW bodies were sound enough to be sold on for further use. The early post war period would see both chassis and body makers busily employed trying to satisfy the demand for new or rebuilt vehicles, including Brush, a body builder able to supply composite bodies (i.e. timber framing strengthened with steel flitch plates) or ones with patented all-metal construction, the aluminium exterior panelling being fastened to wood fillets secured in the steel pillars. Brush were already well established, not only as a bus and coach body builder but in the production of tramcars, those supplied to Blackpool in particular enjoying a long life. However, once the initial post war need for vehicles was met and sales deteriorated,

Brush ceased building bus and coach bodies in 1952. Unfinished vehicles and patents passed to Willowbrook, whose factory was located about a mile away from Brush.

After twenty years of operation by North Western, 728 was finally withdrawn in 1956 and sold to Frank Cowley, the Salford dealer, who had been the major purchaser disposing of North Western vehicles on their withdrawal. The vehicle was sold to a Welsh contractor for use as a site office before being rescued for preservation by David Moores, David's care in keeping 728 in dry secure storage for over fifty years before donating it to the Quantock fleet has resulted in a vehicle which, on initial inspection, appears to still be in sound condition on the body. Unfortunately, however, 728 is minus all its internal fittings.

Far Left
Originally built to become a cinema but for which use a licence was refused, this was the North Western garage in Wilmslow up to 1960. JA 5528 is seen with its 1946 Brush body. The garage could only accommodate eight vehicles, and bigger premises were moved to in 1961. Similar in vintage to the bus, the saloon is possibly a Lanchester.

Left
The Brush 1930s sales promotion catalogue describes both the all-metal as well as the composite methods of construction used by the Company. (Image courtesy of Leicester Arts and Museum Service)

PERIMETER SEATING

There is also one other aspect of the vehicle's history which raises its level of importance in social history. Apart from being converted to run on producer gas, wartime operation saw one further modification, this time involving the seating and carrying capacity on 728's E.C.W. body. Large operators including North Western had to fit a number of single deck vehicles with what was termed perimeter seating. This meant removing existing seating and placing seating longitudinally round the sides of the vehicle, thus reducing the actual seating capacity to around twenty-nine, but with many more standing passengers increasing the carrying capacity overall. This was to try to cope with increasing passenger numbers, particularly on works services, with fewer vehicles. The restoration of 728 would mean it would be one of a very small number of JO5Gs to be restored, with a unique history, and a body made by Brush whose work now is almost as rare as the chassis. It is truly a very rare vehicle.

Above
Now with Quantock Heritage and having been kept under cover for so many years by David Moores, the bodywork on 728 appears to still be in a sound condition, but nothing can be certain until exterior panels are removed.

Left
Brush – now no more, along with so many other body makers who no longer exist.

BRUSH
COACHWORK LIMITED
LOUGHBOROUGH, ENGLAND
Telephone: Telegrams:
LOUGHBOROUGH · 3131.   BRUSH LOUGHBOROUGH.

YESTERDAY'S BUSES

Both Peter and Cliff have long established friendships with Steve. Both have been privileged to be involved with him in historical research, vehicle repair and renovation together with being able to get behind the wheel and drive not only on rallies which Steve has supported but on the vintage services he has operated. Peter has been responsible for the organisation of what in its five years of operation had become a major event in the vintage bus calendar, the Taunton Vintage Bus Day. Cliff has spent much time ferreting around for vehicles which eventually joined the Heritage Fleet.

They share along with Steve not only the desire to preserve vehicles of a bygone age but, by experiencing them, help the public to be aware of their place in social and industrial history.

Back Cover Photo: Rear Ends! (Peter Snowden)

YESTERDAY'S BUSES

INDEX

Make	Model	Year	Body	Original Operator	Registration	Pages
AEC	Regal 1	1946	Beadle OB35F	Maidstone & District	HKL 819	10
	Regal 111	1948	Windover C32F	Trent	ACH 441	80
		1948	Strachan B35R	Crosville	JFM 575	98 to 100
		1948	Burlingham B35F	Gillett Bos. Co. Durham	JUP 233	80
	Regent 111	1949	Park Royal O33/26R	Morecambe & Heysham Corporation	KTF 594	10
	Reliance MU3RV	1956	Burlingham B44F	Safeguard, Guildford	200 APB	79
	Reliance 2MU3RV	1959	Willowbrook C31F	Grey Cars	890 ADV	79
	Regent V 2D3RA	1960	Northern Counties FL37/33F	Barton	851 FNN	61 to 65
	Reliance 2MU3RV	1960	Weymann DP41F	PMT	805 EVT	80
		1961	Weymann OB40F	Maidstone & District (Originally registered 325 NKT)	AFE 719A	10
	Routemaster	1961	Park Royal H36/28R	London Transport (Originally registered as WLT 787)	792 UXA	21
	Reliance 2MU3RV	1963	Alexander DP41F	North Western	RDB 846	74
	Regent V 2D2RA	1966	Neepsend H37/28R	Ipswich Corporation	DPV 65D	46 to 49
Bristol	JO5G	1936	ECW B31R (rebodied 1946 Brush B31R)	North Western	JA 5528	101 to 103
	L5G	1938	ECW B33R (rebodied 1950/1 Burlingham B35R)	North Western	AJA 132	24, 73, 74
	L6A	1948	ECW B35R (later B35F)	Crosville	GFM 882	Front Cover and 5
	L5G	1950	Weymann B35R	North Western	**CDB 205**	75
		1950	Weymann B35R	North Western	CDB 206	73, 74
		1950	ECW B35R	Crosville	KFM 767	5,6

Make	Model	Year	Body	Original Operator	Registration	Pages
Bristol	L5G	1950	ECW B35R	Crosville	KFM 893	5,6
		1950	ECW B35R	Crosville	LFM 717	5,6
	LL5G	1950	ECW B39R	Crosville	LFM 734	5,6
	LS6G	1953	ECW C39F	Royal Blue	OTT 96	78
	LD6G	1956	ECW O33/27R	Southern Vectis	BAS 563	9
		1956	ECW O33/27R	Southern Vectis	BAS 562	9
		1956	ECW O33/27R	Southern Vectis	BAS 564	9
		1957	ECW O33/27RD	Crosville	833 AFM	7, 8
		1957	ECW H33/27RD	Crosville	838 AFM	7 to 9
	LDL6G	1957	ECW O37/33RD	Western National	VDV 752	9, 24
		1957	ECW O37/33RD	Western National	VDV 753	9
	FSF6G	1962	ECW O34/26F	Crosville	891 VFM	7,8
	FLF6G	1965	ECW H38/32F	Hants & Dorset	DEL 893C	80
Crossley	DD42/7	1949	Scottish Commercial L32/25R Rebody 1954 Roe H32/25R	Baxter's, Airdrie Wood, Mirfield	EVD 406	27,28
Daimler	COG5/40	1939	Willowbrook C35F	Blue Bus Services	GNU 750	79
	CWA6	1945	Duple L30/26R	Huddersfield J.O.C.	CCX 777	86 to 94
		1945	Duple L30/26R	Huddersfield J.O.C.	**CCX 778**	83
		1945	Duple L30/26R	London Transport	**HGC 257**	92, 93
		1945	Duple L30/26R	Brown's, Tunstall	**KEH 7 & 8**	90, 91
	CVD6/SD	1950	Willowbrook B35F	Bullocks, Featherstone	CHL 772	79
	CVG6LX-30	1962	Roe H39/31F	Leeds Corporation	572 CNW	79
	Fleetline CRL6	1976	Alexander CO43/31F	Bournemouth Corporation	NFX 134P	12
Dennis	Lancet J3	1949	Park Royal B35R	East Kent	CFN 121	79, 96
Leyland	Titan TD4	1936	Massey L27/26R (rebodied 1949 ECW L27/26R)	Cumberland	BRM 596	66 to 68
	Titan TD5	1936	Massey L27/26R	Cumberland	**DAO 50**	66
	Tiger TS7	1937	Harrington C32R	Southdown	DUF 179	97
	Tiger TS8	1938	Park Royal C32R	East Kent	JG 9938	95, 96

Make	Model	Year	Body	Original Operator	Registration	Pages
Leyland	Titan PD1	1947	Duple L29/26F	Barton	JNN 384	51-2, 54 to 57
	Tiger PS1	1948	Willowbrook L31/30RD (1957)	Barton	WAL 782	58 to 60
	Titan PD1	1948	Duple L29/26F	Barton	**JNN 793**	52
		1948	Duple L29/26F	Barton	**JRR 930**	52
		1948	Duple L29/26F	Barton	**JVO 233**	53
	Titan PD1/3	1948	Burlingham FCL27/22RD	Ribble	**BRN 271**	16
		1948	Burlingham FCL27/22RD	Ribble	**BRN 277**	13. 16
	Tiger PS2/1	1949	Burlingham FC35F	Bournemouth Corporation	JLJ 401/2	11
	Tiger PS1/1	1950	Santus C33F	Bere Regis & District	**CJT 820**	59
		1950	Burlingham C33F	Iveson, Co. Durham	KUP 949	80
		1950	Weymann DP35F (later DP31F)	Crosville	LFM 302	1 to 4
		1950	Weymann DP35F	Crosville	LFM 320	1 to 4
		1950	Weymann DP35F	Crosville	LFM 329	1 to 4
	Titan PD2/3	1950	East Lancs FCL27/22RD	Ribble	**DCK 205**	15
		1950	East Lancs FCL27/22RD	Ribble	**DCK 211**	19
		1950	Weymann H48D	Bournemouth Corporation	KEL 131	12
	Titan PD2/1	1951	Leyland O30/26R	Stockport Corporation	EDB 549	76, 77
	Titan PD2/3	1951	East Lancs FCL27/22RD	Ribble	**DCK 218**	14
		1951	East Lancs FCL27/22RD	Ribble	DCK 219	17 to 20
	Titan PD2/12	1953	Leyland H31/26R	Rawtenstall Corporation	RTC 822	69 to 71
	Royal Tiger PSU1/13	1954	Burlingham B42F	Bournemouth Corporation	NLJ 271	11
	Titan PD2/12	1954	Leyland H32/26R	Barton	RAL 334	70
		1954	Leyland H30/26RD	Scout Motor Services	**STC 887**	70, 71
	Tiger Cub PSUC1/1	1958	Crossley B44F	Stockport Corporation	NDB 356	25, 26
		1960	Willowbrook DP43F	North Western	LDB 796	78
	Titan PD2A/24	1964	East Lancs H35/28R	Blackburn Corporation	ABV 43B	38 to 40, 49
	Titan PD2A/30	1966	East Lancs H32/28R	Eastbourne Corporation	BJK 674D	41, 42, 49
		1966	East Lancs H32/28R	Eastbourne Corporation	BJK 680D	42

Make	Model	Year	Body	Original Operator	Registration	Pages
Leyland	Titan PD3/4	1966	East Lancs H38/32F	Haslingden Corporation	XTF 98D	43 to 45, 49
	Titan PD2/40	1967	East Lancs H36/28R	Stockport Corporation	**HJA 955E**	35
		1967	Neepsend H36/28R	Stockport Corporation	**HJA 956E**	36
		1967	Neepsend H36/28R	Stockport Corporation	HJA 965E	33 to 37, 49
		1967	Neepsend H36/28R	Stockport Corporation	**HJA 968E**	34
Leyland/ Beadle	semi-chassisless TD5	1938/52	Beadle FC35F	East Kent	GFN 273	29, 30
Scania	OmniDekka	2005	East Lancs PO43/26F	Quantock	YN55RDV	22, 23

GENERAL NOTES

- *The index shows all the vehicles that are discussed in this book. Included, and indicated, are a few buses that have not been owned by Quantock but are here because they are part of the story. Non-Quantock owned buses are highlighted* **thus** *above.*

- *Not included are details of the vehicles in the two photos on the Acknowledgements page but adding those to the list above will give some indication of the number of vehicles, their types and the operators which have featured in the Quantock Fleet over the years. As mentioned elsewhere, it has always been Quantock's policy to sell vehicles periodically in order to help finance and restore new purchases. Many vehicles listed above are now with new owners; some of those new owners are mentioned in the text.*

- *This book goes nowhere near covering all the buses that have passed through Quantock's hands but gives a flavour of the rich variety that have. For example, a study of the line ups of buses on the Acknowledgements page will reveal several vehicles that have not been covered in this book.*